DAD LAW

CHRONICLE BOOKS
SAN FRANCISCO

DAD LAW

*The Definitive Reference
for All Things Dad*

written by

ALLY PROBST & JOEL WILLIS
EDITORS OF THE DAD

Library of Congress Cataloging-in-Publication Data available.

ISBN 978-1-7972-2005-5

Manufactured in China.

Design by Evelyn Furuta.

AOL is a registered trademark of Yahoo Inc. Atari is a registered trademark of Atari Interactive, Inc. Band-Aid is a registered trademark of Johnson & Johnson. Beetle is a registered trademark of Volkswagen Aktiengesellschaft. Blockbuster Video is a registered trademark of Blockbuster L.L.C. Bluetooth is a registered trademark of Bluetooth Sig, Inc. Carhartt is a registered trademark of Carhartt, Inc. Crocs is a registered trademark of Crocs, Inc. Disneyland is a registered trademark of Disney Enterprises, Inc. Disney World is a registered trademark of Disney Enterprises, Inc. Facebook is a registered trademark of Meta Platforms, Inc. Fortnite is a registered trademark of Epic Games, Inc. GoldenEye is a registered trademark of Danjaq, LLC. Grammy Awards is a registered trademark of National Academy of Recording Arts & Sciences, Inc. Happy Meal is a registered trademark of McDonald's Corporation. Hot Wheels is a registered trademark of Mattel, Inc. IKEA is a registered trademark of Inter-IKEA Systems B.V. Instagram is a registered trademark of Instagram, LLC. iPad is a registered trademark of Apple Inc. Jeopardy! is a registered trademark of Jeopardy Productions, Inc. Jurassic Park is a registered trademark of Universal City Studios LLC. LEGO is a registered trademark of the LEGO Group. Lincoln Logs is a registered trademark of Hasbro, Inc. Lucky Charms is a registered trademark of General Mills IP Holdings II, LLC. March Madness is a registered trademark of National Collegiate Athletic Association. Mario Kart is a registered trademark of Nintendo of America Inc. McDonald's is a registered trademark of McDonald's Corporation. MTV Cribs is a registered trademark of Viacom International Inc. M&M's is a registered trademark of Mars, Incorporated. New Balance is a registered trademark of New Balance Athletics, Inc. NFL is a registered trademark of National Football League. Nike is a registered trademark of Nike, Inc. Nintendo is a registered trademark of Nintendo of America Inc. Nokia is a registered trademark of Nokia Corporation. NORAD is a registered trademark of Kai U.S.A., Ltd. Pinewood Derby is a registered trademark of Boy Scouts of America. Ping-Pong is a registered trademark of Parker Brothers, Inc. Pong is a registered trademark of Atari Interactive, Inc. Powerball is a registered trademark of Multi-state Lottery Association. Power Wheels is a registered trademark of Mattel, Inc. Pull-Ups is a registered trademark of Kimberly-Clark Worldwide, Inc. Starbucks is a registered trademark of Starbucks Corporation. Star Wars is a registered trademark of Lucasfilm Ltd. Super Bowl is a registered trademark of National Football League. Superman is a registered trademark of DC Comics. Super Mario is a registered trademark of Nintendo of America Inc. Super Soaker is a registered trademark of Hasbro, Inc. Tetris is a registered trademark of Tetris Holding, LLC. TikTok is a registered trademark of ByteDance Ltd. The Crocodile Hunter is a registered trademark of Australia Zoo Pty Ltd. The Elf on the Shelf is a registered trademark of CCA and B, LLC. The Far Side is a registered trademark of FarWorks, Inc. Top Gun is a registered trademark of Top Gun Intellectual Properties, LLC. Trans-Siberian Orchestra is a registered trademark of Trans-Siberian Orchestra, Inc. Walkman is a registered trademark of Sony Corporation. WD-40 is a registered trademark of WD-40 Manufacturing Company. Wi-Fi is a registered trademark of Wi-Fi Alliance.

10 9 8 7 6 5 4 3 2 1

Chronicle books and gifts are available at special quantity discounts to
corporations, professional associations, literacy programs, and other organizations.
For details and discount information, please contact our premiums department at
corporatesales@chroniclebooks.com or at 1-800-759-0190.

Chronicle Books LLC
680 Second Street
San Francisco, California 94107
www.chroniclebooks.com

· CONTENTS ·

· PREFACE ·

All dads since the dawn of time have intuitively understood that there is a set of rules that govern us. An unshakable beacon of ultimate dad truth, it guides men to buy crisp white sneakers and whispers bad puns into their ears. Dad Law is what separates the men from the boys, the dads from the animals.

In the past, these governing laws of fatherhood have been largely unspoken and unwritten, but no more. Now, all dads, old and new alike, may review this extensive volume of Dad Law. Upon reading, dads should adjust themselves accordingly, lest they be found in violation and forced to turn in their cargo shorts. They will be policed by their fellow dads and their internal compass of self-respect.

A dad may enforce Dad Law at any time upon a rival dad, thus cementing himself as #1 Dad and forcing the perpetrator to turn over any mugs, shirts, or hats reflecting this title. Familiarize yourself with Dad Law to protect yourself, your family, and your dad street rep.

DAD AT HOME

· DOMESTIC RESPONSIBILITIES ·

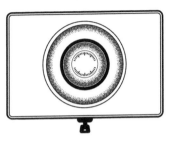

01. *A dad will guard the thermostat, and none shall be permitted to adjust it without first pleading their case and presenting a persuasive argument. Even then, a dad is unlikely to yield.*

02. If a family member states that they are cold and would like to turn the thermostat up, a dad will respond with one of the following rebuttals:
  a. "Go put on a sweater."
  b. "Go to the corner; it's 90 degrees."
  c. "Hi, Cold. I'm Dad."
  d. "You'll live."
  e. "Go run around the block; that'll warm you up."

03. A dad will insist that any person entering his house be "in or out, but close the door." Shutting the door is of utmost importance because he's not paying to heat/cool the whole neighborhood.

04. A dad will tell anyone who leaves a door or window open that they are "letting the flies out."

05. After flipping on a light switch, a dad will say, "Let there be light!" with dramatic flair.

06. A dad will complain that he's the only one who ever turns lights off in this house.
   a. He will constantly remind members of his household that when they leave a room, they should turn the lights off.
   b. If he finds a room with many lights on, a dad will comment, "It looks like Las Vegas in here!"
   c. Occasionally a dad will rhetorically ask his family if they own stock in the electric company.

07. In the event that someone has had the refrigerator open for more than two minutes, a dad must tell the perpetrator to close it so they "don't let all the cold air out."

08. A dad will ask a kid standing in front of the open fridge door if they are "waiting for penguins."

09. A dad at home is required to be on call to open difficult jars at any time, should the need arise.

    a. After doing so, a dad will tell the person needing assistance, "You must've loosened it for me."

    b. A dad may also flex his biceps after opening the jar and may choose to refer to them as "guns."

10. A dad is responsible for taking the garbage out because no one else will do it. He will continue to do it (with or without complaining, depending on the day) until the day he has a child of appropriate age to complete the job, at which point he will switch to telling the kid to do it.

11. At some point in his adult life, a dad may find he actually enjoys taking out the trash because stepping outside is a nice little break all to himself. After depositing the trash in the receptacle, he may linger outside, enjoying the blissful lack of kid noise for a moment. This is a dad secret that is not to be shared under any circumstances or risk ruining the sanctity of trash-break time.

12. A dad will be called in to handle all urgent toilet plunging situations, regardless of how terrifying they may be.

13. A dad will investigate any mysterious sounds (real or imagined) reported by members of his family at night. It's a spooky job but someone's gotta do it.

· BUG REMOVAL ·

14. If an insect is found trespassing on the family's private residence, a dad will lead the bug removal response. In doing so, he will follow the approved procedure:

    a. A dad will tell the family, "It's more afraid of you than you are of it."

    b. He will pretend that he is not afraid of it, even if he secretly is.

    c. He will attempt to identify the bug and make a judgment of its innocence if it's not a dangerous type (e.g., "That's just a mosquito eater. He's ugly as sin but he won't hurtchya.").

    d. A dad will try to politely relocate the bug off his property, if possible.

    e. He will apologize to the creature (e.g., "Sorry, little buddy, but you gotta go. You don't pay rent and these guys want you out.").

    f. If unable to cordially escort the intruding bug off his property, a dad may be forced to terminate it. In the event that a dad must kill a bug in self-defense, he will *not* scream, even if/when it runs at him in a

14.
(cont.) really creepy way or makes a gross crunch sound when he hits it with his shoe.

    g. He will announce to the entire house that the ordeal is over, he has killed the bug in question, and everyone may come out of hiding.

    h. A dad who has rendered a room bug free will be lauded as a hero.

· PET OWNERSHIP ·

15. A dad who owns a dog will do all of the following:

    a. A dad will fall in love with and spoil the family dog, even if he originally claimed he did not want a dog. Dads cannot resist dogs.

    b. A dad will tell the dog he has the good life: No work and lying around all day getting belly rubs is the dream. A dad may also tease a lazy dog that he "must've had *such* a hard day" when he knows the dog has been lying on the couch all day.

    c. A dad will sneak the dog table scraps even though he knows he's not supposed to, and he said he wouldn't do that anymore.

    d. A dad will end each dog petting session by giving the dog three quick pats on the side. This communicates to the dog that he's a good boy/girl but it's time to move along now.

15.   **e.**   A dad will be sure to always ask the dog if he/she
(cont.)   knows who's a good boy/girl several times a day.

      f.   A dad will fondly refer to a family dog with an
         affectionate but derogatory nickname such as:

           i.   "you mangy mutt"

           ii.   "you furball"

           iii. "you big goof"

           iv.   "you lazy bag of bones"

16.   If a dad owns a cat, similar laws apply but are adapted to the temperament of the animal. If a dad is not a "cat person" and attempts to respectfully keep his distance from the animal, the cat will likely end up loving him even more, which is entertaining for the other members of the household to watch.

17.   *If a dad buys his kid a fish, he may be responsible either for emergency runs back to the pet store to replace the fish before his kid notices it is dead or the hosting of a fish funeral around a toilet bowl. A dad will always have a fish eulogy in the back of his mind, ready to pull out as needed.*

· CLEANING ·

18. If a dad sees that his spouse has begun "rage cleaning" (defined as: frantically cleaning the entire house with the intensity of a thousand suns), he has two choices:

    a. start cleaning and attempt to at least match, if not exceed, his spouse's rage

    b. make himself as scarce as possible

    (In either case, he's required to make legitimate attempts to get the kids to help.)

19. A dad cleaning the house will do one or more of the following:

    a. carry a trash bag around and say, "The next time I find (Exhibit A: random object) on the floor, it's going straight into the trash."

    b. joke that it's time to sell the house and get a new one

    c. say, "This room looks like it was hit by a tornado."

    d. say, "Many hands make light work," in an attempt to guilt more people into helping

    e. say, "No wonder we can never find anything in this house!"

    f. warn, "There's gonna be some changes around here!" He's not sure what those changes may be, but he knows they are coming.

19.
(cont.)
   g. call a messy room a "pigsty"

   h. tell any kids complaining about chores that the whole reason he had kids was for the free labor

20. If a member of the family can't locate something, a dad will tease them, saying, "You'd lose your head if it wasn't screwed on!" (Although a dad will say this, he will not permit it to be said back to him the next time he loses something.)

21. If a kid is having trouble finding something that's right in front of their face, a dad will say, "If it was a snake, it would've bitten you."

22. If a kid is searching for a specific item in the house, a dad will "help" by doing one of the following:

   a. asking, "Where's the last place you had it?"

   b. telling the kid to retrace their steps

   c. reminding the kid this wouldn't happen if they kept their room clean

   d. saying, "The first step to finding it is cleaning up."

   e. stating, "It's always in the last place you look."

23. If a dad finds that a member of the family has left food or garbage out somewhere in the house, he will ask, "Do you want ants? Because this is how you get ants."

· DISHES ·

24. A dad charged with doing the dishes will leave several dishes, if not all of them, in the sink "to soak." Let the record state that this counts as completing the task, in his mind.

25. *A dad unloading the dishwasher will remind his family that they shouldn't run knives through the dishwasher because it dulls them. He may also have thoughts on the only correct way to load the dishwasher, which he will share with anyone within earshot.*

26. A dad will own a knife sharpener and feel like a badass ninja when sharpening kitchen knives with it. A dad is only as sharp as his dullest knife.

27. A dad searching for a lid to a plastic storage container will always complain about how hard it is to find the matching lid for a given container. Opening the drawer containing all the lids may result in justified swearing.

· BATHROOM PROTOCOL ·

28. When in need of a break from his family or a safe haven from doing the dishes, a dad will hide in the bathroom until the situation is deemed safe enough for him to emerge or his spouse demands his reappearance, whichever comes first.

29. Despite the fact that a dad may stay in the bathroom for wildly long stretches himself, if someone else has been in the bathroom for an amount of time deemed even slightly excessive, a dad will ask, "What, did you fall in?"

30. After using the shower, a dad will complain about one or more of the following:
    a. the amount of hair in the drain
    b. the number of shampoo bottles and assorted toiletry products sitting around in there
    c. In the case of a large family, he may state annoyance that everyone "used all the hot water."

31. If someone says, "I'm going to take a shower," a dad will respond with, "Make sure to put it back when you're done!"

32. A dad's bodily functions are all louder than necessary, but his sneeze shall be loud enough to shake the foundation of the house.

33. A dad will make a strangely haunting foghorn sound when he blows his nose. It is a great unexplained medical mystery how a dad manages to do this, but it is required. (It is mandated that the volume will increase with a dad's age.)

34. A dad using the toilet will make use of "courtesy flushes" and will warn members of his family to steer clear of the bathroom after he's been in there, if necessary.

35. A dad will use candles and/or air freshener if they are available to him, or he may suggest the need to "light a match." This shows he is considerate of his family's well-being.

36. A dad will keep reading material in the bathroom lest he be caught in there with nothing to do but read the back of the shampoo bottle.

· DESIGNATED DAD AREAS ·

37.   A dad may put in a request to have a designated area such as a study, shop, garage, "man cave," or gaming setup where he can display decor deemed unsuitable for the rest of the house. Depending on the dad's personality and interests, it may include:

  a. video game paraphernalia
  b. sports team paraphernalia
  c. fancy leather-bound books and at least one antique globe or map
  d. neon signs (especially, but not limited to, light-up beer signs)
  e. camouflage or hunting paraphernalia
  f. movie theater paraphernalia (especially, but not limited to, '90s movie posters, a popcorn machine that is used only twice a year, an unnecessarily large screen)
  g. a bar area or liquor cabinet
  h. games such as pinball, darts, pool, foosball, Ping-Pong, etc.

This designated dad area, if approved by his spouse, will be respected as a sacred space. The dad will maintain complete control of this area, up to and until his spouse tells him he needs to change something, in which case he will probably just yield.

· OVERHEARD AT HOME ·

38. A dad who bumps into a wall that has always been in his house will ask, "Who put that wall there?"

39. A dad will regularly remind his children that he owns the roof. Examples of this include but are not limited to:
   a. "As long as you're under my roof, you'll live by my rules."
   b. "I put a roof over your head."

40. At any time, and often without warning, a dad may refer to his home as:
   a. "Casa de (family name)"
   b. "my crib" (He will insist that this is cool slang like they use on *MTV Cribs* and will not be swayed by family members complaining it's embarrassing when he calls it that.)
   c. "the homestead"

41. A dad departing his home will implore remaining family members to "hold down the fort."

DAD IN PUBLIC

· ARRIVALS AND DEPARTURES ·

01. Dads must arrive at all locations and events early in order to "beat the rush." Arriving anywhere at the same time as "the rush" is against Dad Law. "The rush" is for fools with poor time management.

02. When a dad beats the rush and a line forms behind him, he will smugly inform his party, "We got here just in time."

03. Dads will leave any/all public events early in order to "beat the traffic." A dad will even go so far as to leave a sporting event without knowing the final score as long as it means he will not have to wait around in the parking lot of the stadium trying to exit. Missing the end of the event for which he probably paid good money is a price he's willing to pay for dignity.

04. When a dad is ready to leave, he will indicate it by suggesting, at minimum, one of the following:
   a. "Let's rock and roll."
   b. "Let's hit the road."
   c. "Let's blow this popsicle stand." (No dad knows the origin of the mythical "popsicle stand"; he only knows he wants to blow it.)
   d. "Saddle up, partners."

04.
(cont.)
  e. "Let's get the heck outta Dodge!"
  f. "Let's get this show on the road."
  g. "Let's skedaddle."
  h. "Let's put the pedal to the metal."
  i. "Let's hightail it out of here."
  j. "Let's make like a tree and leave."

05. If a dad hears another dad say, "Let's hit the road," he must retort, "What did the road ever do to you?" This is a classic way to out-dad a dad at his own game.

ETA
ESTIMATED TIME *of* ARRIVAL

06. *If a dad was meant to meet someone and the person in question is more than three minutes late, the dad must call him and ask for his "ETA." If you didn't want him to call and hassle you, you should have been on time.*

07. An enthusiastic dad hug will always end with a quick three pats on the back. The three pats signal to the other person that hug time has ended. Wrap it up.

· GROCERY SHOPPING ·

08. *A dad sent to the store for specific items will never take a list. He will tell everyone (and himself) that he will remember all the needed items. Once in the store, however, a dad is easily distracted, and his memory fails him. He will forget at least two items, often including the main one for which he was sent.*

09. A dad who returns home from the store with several missing items must turn right around and go back to get them or else face the wrath of family members who told him to write the list down.

10. A dad who is unsure of which brand or type of item his family wants him to get will call them from the store to confirm the specifications. Often this means several phone calls and a lot of standing around in the aisles trying to ascertain the differences between two things that seem exactly the same but are marked with different prices. If he is unable to get an answer, he will default to the cheaper product. If they don't like it, they can get it themselves next time.

11.   If a cashier has trouble scanning an item, a dad must state, "Guess it's free then." An accompanying wink is suggested, though not required, by Dad Law.

12.   If a cashier asks a dad if he would like his milk in a bag, a dad must respond, "No, you can just leave it in the carton." He will then look around to see if anyone else caught this brilliant retort. If the cashier laughs, the dad will go to that cashier's lane every time thereafter.

13.   If a grocery store changes its layout at any point, a dad will voice a verbal complaint and appear outwardly distressed. He had just gotten used to the last layout, and this one is all wrong. How is he expected to find anything now?

14.   A dad coming out of the grocery store will pass off his shopping cart to an incoming dad and state, "I left some gas in it for ya."

· INTERACTING WITH FRIENDS ·

15.   Upon running into a fellow dad or friend, a dad must greet him with one or more of the following statements:
      a. "Look at this guy!"
      b. "Who let this guy in here?"
      c. "I guess they're just letting anyone in here now."

15.   **d.** "Uh oh, here comes trouble!"
(cont.)   **e.** "Look out for this one."

      f. "Hey, stranger."

      g. "Long time no see!" (Only applicable if the friend and the dad have very recently been in close proximity. It is meant as a joke, not a genuine sentiment.)

      h. "Well, well, well. Look what the cat dragged in."

      i. "Aren't you a sight for sore eyes!" (This is the highest of dad compliments, reserved for very old friends.)

      j. "Well, you son of a gun!" (Being called a "son of a gun" by a dad is an honor and should be treated as such.)

16.   A dad will say, "Fancy meeting you here" to a person with whom he had planned on meeting.

17.   If a dad encounters a friend at a store, he will come up behind him and tell a store employee, "Don't take this guy's money. It's no good."

18.   A dad running into an old friend will tease him about how terrible/old he looks. A dad telling a friend he looks terrible is a sign of affection.

19.   If a dad finds out that a friend is going to be a father for the first time, he will wish him an official, "Welcome to the club," including a supportive back pat. Dads love welcoming more into the club.

20. If someone asks a dad "How's it going?" it is against Dad Law for a dad to reply with a real answer. Instead, he must respond with one of the following:

    a. "Oh, it's goin'!"

    b. "Livin' the dream."

21. If a dad is greeted with "Good to see you!" he may wow the other person with a hilarious reply of "Good to be seen!"

22. A dad describing an old friend will say, "We went to separate schools together."

23. A dad saying goodbye to a friend will say one or more of the following:

    a. "Don't be a stranger."

    b. "Have your people call my people."

    c. "You take care of yourself now."

24. A dad will ask, "Trouble in paradise?" when a friend gets off the phone with his rock-solid spouse. It's meant as a joke. A dad would never ask this of a friend with a shaky marriage.

25. A dad will have at least one friend from high school or college who has a crazy nickname and still comes up in conversation regularly fifteen-plus years later. The stories about this guy are epic. Want to know the explanation of that crazy nickname? You had to be there.

· INTERACTING WITH STRANGERS ·

26. When engaging with anyone significantly older than he is, a dad may refer to that individual as "young man"/"young lady."

27. If a dad encounters a person walking a large dog on a leash, the required statement is "Looks more like the dog is walking you!" This statement should be repeated at a louder volume if it seems the stranger did not hear or acknowledge the hilarity of it.

28. If a dad sees someone get carded, he will ask, "Would you like to see my ID too?" This is funnier the older the dad is.

29. If someone tells a dad his kid is cute, he will respond, "Yeah, I think we'll keep him/her."

30. If a dad expects a lot of people to be in attendance at an event, he will say, "Everyone and their mother will be there." You do *not* want to be somewhere at the same time as everyone and their mother. They're part of "the rush." (See Section II, Article 1.)

31. A dad using an automatic door will do one or more of the following:

   a. pretend he's using The Force to open the door

   b. jokingly tell the person behind him, "Let me get the door for ya."

· GROUPS AND FAMILY ·

32. If a dad is with a group that decides to walk somewhere, a dad must say, "Guess we're hoofin' it."

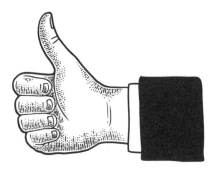

33. *A dad in a new place that he likes (including, but not limited to, a new brewery, a car wash with free popcorn, a restaurant with free refills, and a bar playing music that he likes) will voice his approval by stating, "Now this is my kinda place."*

34. When using the bathroom at a bar or brewery, a dad will casually comment, "You don't buy beer, you rent it."

35. A dad will sneak as many random facts into casual conversation as possible. He may preface these by saying, "Fun fact . . . ," even though the fact is not fun at all. It's a dad's calling to share information that nobody asked for.

36. When speaking to an individual who has recently had a noticeable haircut, a dad is required by Dad Law to make a comment on it. He will remark one of the following:
   a. "Lookin' sharp."
   b. "Looks like you got your ears lowered."
   c. "You look great. I didn't recognize you." This is often accompanied by a gentle elbow nudge to indicate he's just teasing you.
   d. "You got a haircut . . .
      i. Which one?"
      ii. Why not get all of them cut?"

37. A dad is required to bring attention to any building and/or storefront that a now-obsolete business used to occupy and subsequently marvel about the passage of time (e.g., "I remember when this was a Blockbuster Video!").

38. A dad who observes his neighbor washing his car is required to ask, "Can you do mine next?" (The same procedure is also required for a neighbor shoveling snow. See Section XIII, Article 11.)

39. A dad wishing to get out of a previously agreed-upon social gathering of any kind is permitted to use his kids as an excuse not to go. If a dad states that he can't go because of his kids, none shall argue with him.

DAD IN THE CAR

· FAMILY ·

01. *If kids are misbehaving in the back seat, a dad will threaten to "turn this car around."*

02. A dad at the wheel has complete control over the music playing in his car, except in the case of:
    a. a baby who is crying and only calms down to the *Moana* soundtrack
    b. a spouse asking to listen to something else

03. A dad who has forgotten his car keys will return for them and then say, "Can't get very far without these."

04. Before a kid gets in the car, a dad must say, "Saddle up, partner."

05. A dad will allow a kid to back the car down the driveway at least one year before they are ready for it.

06. At long stoplights, a dad must watch cross streetlights and pretend to be able to make his light turn green at just the right time. If a kid asks how he did it, he's not allowed to say. A magician never reveals his secrets.

07. When crossing train tracks, a dad must say, "Ya know how I know a train has been here? It left its tracks."

08. If a family member walks in front of their parked car, a dad will honk the horn to make them jump. This is always funny.

09. If a dad is waiting in the driveway or picking up a passenger, as the passenger approaches he's required to scoot the car up just a little. This may go on five to ten more times, or until it stops getting a laugh. And then one more time.

10. If a dad is standing outside a car, talking to someone in that car, he will wrap up the conversation and wish them goodbye and safe journey with two quick pats on the roof of the car before they drive off.

11. To scare kids into turning off an annoying dome light at night, dads will tell them that it's illegal to keep it on and they don't want to get pulled over.

12. A dad will warn his family that if they need to use the bathroom they'd better do it now because he's not stopping again.

13. When driving in heavy rain conditions a dad must pretend, through the use of magic, that he's able to stop the rain while driving under an overpass.

· CRITIQUING OTHER DRIVERS ·

14. Swear words spoken in the car don't count. Especially when the other guy really deserved it.

15. A dad will say, "People don't know how to drive in this town," no matter what town he is in.

16. If a dad is at a stoplight that turns green, and the car in front of him stays stationary, even if only for a fraction of a second, a dad shall do one or more of the following:
    a. say, "Light's green!"
    b. immediately honk
    c. say, "It's not going to get any greener."
    d. complain, "The guy's probably on his phone."

17. When encountering a bad parking job, a dad will say, "Nice parking job." This is the highest of dad insults.

18. Similarly, when a dad notices someone not using a turn signal, he must say, "Nice turn signal." There's nothing nice about it.

19. In snowy or adverse weather conditions of any kind, a dad will complain that no one knows how to drive in this particular type of weather.

· OBSERVATIONS ·

20. After tying stuff down on a truck, a dad must declare, "That's not going anywhere," before he is permitted to drive.

21. Upon arrival in a new town, a dad will comment on the price of gas and compare it to his hometown. Should the price difference be negligible, he will report on how low gas prices were in 1998.

22. When driving past a cemetery, a dad will typically comment, "People are dying to get in there." Advanced dad procedure allows for dads to refer to the cemetery as "the dead center of town."

23. When a dad sees heavy traffic on a road he's not traveling on, he's expected to say, "Glad we're not going that way!" or, "Good thing we're not over there!"

24. If a dashboard notification says a door is ajar, especially if a passenger makes note of it, a dad must say, "The door is not a jar. The door is a door."

25. It's a dad's duty to report the location of any police officers spotted giving out speeding tickets to everyone he sees for the next week. This is a public service.

26. If a dad gets a speeding ticket, he'll remind you every time he drives past that spot that it is a "speed trap."

27. A dad who does not hit traffic or unexpected obstacles will brag that he is "making good time." "Good time" is a dad's favorite kind of time.

28. If a dad sees a Volkswagen Beetle on the road, he will punch you in the arm in the tradition of "slug bug" (also known as "punch buggy," depending on the state).

29. A dad driving past horses is required to say, "Oh look, horses." Driving past horses without commenting on them is expressly prohibited.

30. When driving past cows in a field, a dad must declare the cows to be "out standing in their field." It does not matter if he has already made this joke fifty times; he is required to do it in any/all cow/field situations.

Ha!

31. *When driving past a cow that is lying down, a dad will refer to it as "ground beef."*

32. If an insect collides with the windshield of a dad's car, he must say, "I bet he doesn't have the guts to do that again."

33. When driving past a newly constructed building, a dad will comment, "Wow, that went up fast."

34. A dad seeing an airplane fly over will comment one or more of the following:
   a. "Where do you think they're headed?"
   b. "That looks low."
   c. "Who can tell me what kind of plane that is?" (He already knows the answer.)

· DIRECTIONS AND ETA ·

35. A dad will not, under any circumstances, voluntarily ask for directions. He will find the way himself or die trying.

36. A dad who is lost while driving will state that he is simply "taking the scenic route."

37. A dad will attempt to beat the Google Maps estimated arrival time. When he is successful, he is required to inform each person he interacts with so that they may be adequately impressed.

38. A dad will give people detailed directions to their destinations, apparently forgetting that everyone just uses their phone to navigate.

39. A dad will plan to arrive at his destination early, as it is a violation of Dad Law to be even five minutes late. (See "beat the rush," Section II, Article 1.)

· REMINISCING ·

40. A dad will tell his kids about the days before power windows, when he had massive muscles from rolling down the windows the old-school way.

41. A dad will tell his kids how inexpensive and junky his first car was but seem oddly sentimental about it. (Every dad's first car had a nickname like "Red Rocket" or "Silver Bullet.")

42. A dad driving through a busy part of town will say, "I remember when this used to all be fields."

· MAINTENANCE AND REPAIR ·

43. A dad can learn everything he needs to know about the state of a tire by kicking it.

44. A dad will always be prepared to offer a lecture on the merits of learning to drive a stick shift. It's a dying art.

45. A dad will remind his family of the importance of wiper fluid and good wiper blades.

46. A dad will insist on changing his car's oil every 3,000 miles, even if the manual says every 6,000 miles. He will ask you every 1,000 miles when you last changed yours.

47. A dad who does not know exactly what's wrong with a given car will declare, "Sounds like the alternator."

48. Observing any damage to a car, a dad trying to be helpful will suggest that maybe it will "buff out" even if it definitely won't buff out.

49. A dad will call taking a car in for routine maintenance a "tune-up."

50. A dad will point out that new models of cars are all run by computers, which is why he can't fix them himself.

51. *A dad will preach the financial advantages of buying a pre-owned car but, even so, will find it hard to resist a brand-new truck.*

52. A dad who wants to justify buying a truck will make up wild scenarios in his mind about all the things he might hypothetically need to haul one day.

· VEHICLE OPERATION ·

53. Parking:

    a. A dad will back into a parking spot even if he can easily pull in front first.

    b. A dad will pass up a close parking spot in the hopes of finding a closer one.

    c. Should he find a better parking spot, a dad must inform everyone he encounters for the next thirty minutes.

54. A dad attempting a difficult driving maneuver, such as parallel parking, looking for a specific turn, or changing lanes in heavy traffic, will turn the radio down while doing it.

55. In order to mark how far to pull the car into the garage, a dad may hang an object such as a tennis ball on a string from the ceiling. He will feel like a genius for doing so.

56. When backing out of the driveway, a dad will put his right arm on the passenger headrest and stare sternly out of the rear window, even if the car has a backup camera. You can't trust those things.

57. On a sunny day, a dad will roll down his driver's side window and rest his elbow in the window opening.

DAD AND MONEY

· FINANCIAL ADVICE AND PRINCIPLES ·

01. A dad is required to remind his family and anyone who will listen, "Money doesn't grow on trees," on at least a weekly or biweekly basis.

02. A dad, contrary to popular belief, is not made of money. He will remind you of this fact if you seem to forget.

03. *A dad who gives his kid a small amount of money will say, "Don't spend it all in one place."*

04. A dad will always wisely state, "If it seems too good to be true, it is."

05. A dad will always read the fine print and remind his family to do the same. There's a sucker born every minute, but he's not one of them.

06. A dad does not respect anyone who doesn't "put their money where their mouth is."

07. A dad will decline any additional warranty protection because that's how they get you.

08. A dad loves anything free but somehow also believes "there's nothing free in this world."

· SPENDING HABITS ·

09. A dad will regularly complain about shopping and/or spending money. The main exception to this is when spending money in a home improvement store, in which case he will not complain.

10. A dad prefers buying in bulk because you get more "bang for your buck."

11. A dad will use the same wallet for his entire adult life.
   a. It will be overstuffed.
   b. It will be leather.
   c. It will be in the back pocket of his jeans at all times.

12. A dad will save every receipt from the last twenty-five years. You never know when you might need that Radio Shack receipt.

13. If a neighbor or friend has purchased a new item (including but not limited to a boat, motorcycle, or riding lawn mower), even the most frugal of dads will say, "I gotta get me one of those."

14. A dad must always have either:
    a. a recently purchased new TV that he tells everyone about
    b. a plan to purchase a new TV in the near future that he consults everyone about

15. A dad will resist his family buying designer or brand-name items by stating that he feels they are overpriced, and a similar item could be purchased for much less. However, he will make exceptions to this for the brands he likes (Nike, Carhartt, etc.), about which he will say, "You get what you pay for."

· BILLS AND OUTGOING EXPENSES ·

16. When purchasing an item, a dad will ask the cashier, "How much do you owe me?"

17. A dad will ask, "What's the damage?" before reading a bill.

18. If a dad thinks something is too expensive, he will say it's practically highway robbery.

19. A dad given a larger than expected total by a cashier may fake a small heart attack to communicate his disapproval.

20. A dad hearing a high price will respond with a low whistle of amazement.

21. If a dad judges an item to be too expensive, he will say it costs "an arm and a leg."

22. A dad will refer to almost any amount of money as a "nice chunk of change."

23. Before making a big purchase, a dad will say he needs some time to "crunch the numbers." The numbers aren't going to crunch themselves.

24. When forced to pay a large amount of money for something, a dad will complain that he's "paying through the nose."

25. A dad will joke that wildly expensive things are "a little out of (his) price range right now."

26. When a dad is drawing the line against something overpriced, he will say, "You've got another think coming" if you think he's going to pay that much.

27. A cynical dad will say, "If you believe that, I've got some oceanfront property in Arizona to sell you."

· THRIFTINESS ·

28. A dad will remind his family to "waste not, want not."

29. A dad will attempt to save money by tearing paper towels in half so a roll will last longer.

30. A dad will refuse expensive shampoo and will instead use the cheapest type of three-in-one shampoo/conditioner/body wash available to him.

31. A dad will skimp on household products, with the one exception being toilet paper. A dad will never buy cheap toilet paper or toilet paper that is less than three-ply. He's not an animal.

32. A dad will always know the current Powerball jackpot down to the dollar, even if he would never buy a ticket.

· FINANCIAL TERMINOLOGY ·

33. If someone has found an easy way to make money, a dad will say he's "on the gravy train."

34. After negotiating for anything, a dad will compliment the other party by saying they "drive a hard bargain."

35. A dad will describe someone he sees as wealthier than himself as one or more of the following:
   a. having "deep pockets"
   b. "not hurting for money"
   c. "doing quite well for himself"

36. A dad will refer to accountants or other financial professionals as "bean counters."

DAD AND FOOD

· HUNGRY DAD ·

01. A hungry dad will say it's time to "rustle up some grub."

02. A dad will say you can call him anything as long as you don't call him late for dinner.

03. If a hostess or waitperson asks, "How are we doing tonight?" a dad will answer, "Hungry!"

04. If anything on anyone else's plate looks particularly appetizing to a dad, he will take a bite and say he is "just testing to see if it's poisonous."

05. A dad will eat any snacks/treats left unattended unless written notice is provided designating them for some greater purpose (e.g., "These cookies are for preschool snack. *Do not eat.*"). If the cookies are designated with a written note, he will try not to eat them. He will not always be successful, but he will try.

· RESTAURANTS ·

06. If a restaurant is packed and there's a wait longer than five minutes, a dad must complain about whoever took the longest to get ready. The delay surely prevented them from beating the rush. (See Section II, Article 1.)

07. If a hostess asks a dad if he has reservations, he must respond, "Yeah, but I came anyway."

08. If a restaurant is completely packed, or completely empty, a dad shall say, "Good thing we made reservations."

09. A dad will complain that the music is too loud in a restaurant, regardless of whether it actually is. If the volume is not an issue, then a dad will complain about the type of music played.

10. Upon receiving the bill at a restaurant, a dad will say one or both of the following statements:
   a. "You got this one?" while passing the bill to a child.
   b. "I guess we're washing dishes!"

11. If a dad witnesses someone ordering a steak well-done, he will inform the offender that they might as well eat a piece of charcoal because they've ruined the meat.

12. When seated at a wobbly restaurant table, it's a dad's duty to attempt to stabilize it with napkins, coasters, or anything else he can "jimmy" in there.

13. When departing a restaurant, a dad must take a complimentary toothpick and walk around feeling like a tough guy with it hanging out of his mouth.

14. A dad will always partake of free mints from the hostess stand.

· SERVER INTERACTIONS ·

15. A dad must treat the task of making the waitstaff laugh as one of utmost urgency. He will stop at nothing to make them laugh, even if it means being blind to his family's annoyance. He will forget that the server is only laughing because it's their job and will take it as irrefutable proof that he is, in fact, very funny.

16. When the waiter introduces themself and says, "I'll be your waiter," a dad will always reply by stating his own name followed by, "I'll be your customer."

17. When ordering food, a dad will confirm the end of his order with a confident "That'll do it."

18. It is required for dads to say, "I better not, I'm driving," when the waitperson offers them a refill of a nonalcoholic drink. This may or may not be paired with a wink.

19. If a waitperson accidentally brings food that was meant for a different table, a dad will hilariously say, "We didn't order that, but we'll take it!"

· EATING ·

20. When the family has ordered way too much food, a dad must joke that he hopes they got enough food.

21. When everyone is enjoying their meal, a dad will say, "Food must be good, everyone got quiet."

22. If a dad witnesses a child using what is deemed to be a more-than-adequate amount of ketchup for their food, he will ask, "Do you want some fries with that ketchup?"

23. A dad who doesn't love his food will say, "It's nothing to write home about."

24. If a kid at the dinner table asks for more of a dad's favorite dish, the dad will joke that it's all gone or he's keeping it all for himself.

· COFFEE SHOPS ·

25. A dad in a coffee shop will act overwhelmed by the myriad options.

26. A dad will choose the plainest black coffee he can obtain and will openly look down on those who order elaborate drinks. (He may secretly think they look delicious but fear ordering them because he doesn't understand what all the variations mean.)

Small ~~Tall~~   ~~Venti~~ Large

27. *A dad must never use Starbucks-specific terms for sizes (tall, grande, venti) but must instead insist on only "small" or "large."*

· FULL DAD ·

28. A dad who has eaten a large amount will:
    a. tell his family, "You're gonna have to roll me out of here."
    b. unbuckle his belt
    c. let out a thirty-second sigh
    d. say, "I can die happy now."
    e. declare the restaurant to be "good eats"

29. After eating, a dad must jokingly declare, "It wasn't good at all," when the waitperson comes to clear his completely empty plate.

30. A dad may say that a delicious meal in a restaurant was good but "not as good as my wife makes."

31. If a waitperson sets him up with, "Do you want a box for that?" a dad will respond, "No, but I'll wrestle you for it." This is a dad joke slam dunk.

32. If offered a second serving of food, a dad will happily respond, "OK, if you twist my arm."

33. A dad leaving somewhere with good treats or food will take "one for the road." The road is long and full of hunger.

34. A dad will tell a kid who didn't finish their meal that clearly their eyes were bigger than their stomach.

35. A dad will finish any/all food left on his kid's plate so that nothing goes to waste and also because 95 percent of the time it's chicken nuggets or mac and cheese, which are delicious. It's a scientific fact that the calories from a kid's leftovers don't count.

36. After burping, a dad will say:

    a. "You know, that's a compliment in some countries."

    b. "Better out than in."

    c. "Tastes better coming up than it did going down."

· PIZZA ·

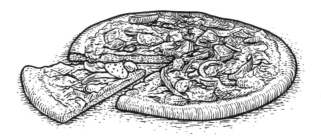

37. *If anyone ever poses the question, "Should we just order pizza?" a dad will respond, enthusiastically, in the affirmative.*

38. A dad will pretend pizza night is a treat for the kids and not just what it actually is: a break from cooking and doing dishes for the parents.

39. When food is delivered to a dad at his home, he's required to make small talk with the delivery person, most commonly inquiring, "Busy night?"

40. When a dad brings in the delivered pizza, he will pretend it is all for him and no one else could possibly want any in order to elicit an outraged reaction that only he finds funny.

41. A dad in proximity to a child with pizza must inform him, "The crust is the best part!"

42. When offered a food he shouldn't have, a dad will respond with:
   a. "No thanks, I'm trying to quit."
   b. "I'm watching my figure." This is often paired with a belly pat.

· BREAKFAST FOODS ·

43. A dad on a weekend will do one of the following:
   a. surprise the kids with donuts
   b. make waffles/pancakes in his pajamas while listening to his favorite album

44. When preparing pancakes, a dad is required to consume the pancakes judged to be weird, burnt, or "icky" himself, thus leaving the higher-quality pancakes for his kids.

45. A dad making pancakes will use his spatula with flair and is encouraged to attempt a fancy flip move. If he misses and the pancake falls on the floor, the dog gets breakfast too.

46. A dad will make and serve bacon whenever possible. Dads love bacon. (Vegetarian dads are exempt from this law, of course.)

· FAST FOOD ·

47. If a child asks to go to the drive-through, a dad will remind them, "We have food at home." He will not let the child know that secretly he would also prefer to go to the drive-through, because the food at home will never compare.

48. A dad at McDonald's will jokingly ask the kid if he wants a Happy Meal or a sad meal.

49. A dad is entitled to collect a fast food "dad tax" of:
    a. one chicken nugget from the kid's meal
    b. a few french fries from the kid's meal
    c. all of the extra fries that fell into the bag, also known as "bonus fries"

50. If a dad comes back with two ice cream cones, he will pretend they're both for him and ask his kid, "Oh, did you want one?"

· IN THE KITCHEN ·

51. When cooking or doing the dishes, a dad who means business will sling a dish towel over his shoulder. A meal cooked by a dad with a towel on his shoulder just tastes better.

52. A dad in the presence of any kind of cheese will make at least one "cut the cheese" joke. He will act as if this is groundbreaking comedy.

53. A dad warming something in the microwave will say he's "nuking it."

54. A dad who feels he makes a good grilled cheese will tell everyone he makes a "mean" grilled cheese.

55. If a kid asks, "What's for dinner?" a dad will not respond seriously but will joke that it's something ridiculous, including but not limited to one of the following options:
    a. liver and onions
    b. anchovies
    c. hot dog water
    d. simply "food"

56. If a child asks, "Can you make me a sandwich?" a dad will respond with elaborate magician moves and then state, "*Poof!* You're a sandwich."

57. A dad must have a trademark chili recipe that he will claim is:

    a. "world-famous"

    b. "award-winning"

despite having no credentials to prove either claim.

58. A dad will leave the oven cracked after cooking something to take advantage of the free heat.

· GRILLING ·

59. *A dad must never allow weather conditions to stop him from grilling.*

60. A dad must publicly declare that he is "firing up the grill" before he may begin grilling.

61. A dad will never intentionally cook a well-done steak.

62. When asking someone how they want their steak cooked, a dad will ask, "You want yours done well, or well-done?"

63. If a dad accidentally burns something to a crisp, he will say it's a little well-done and/or just a little over.

64. A dad will have a trademark marinade, seasoning, and/or method for grilling meat. This is the scent by which he would be identified in nature.

65. A dad must wear an apron to grill. No exceptions. Even if it's just hot dogs. A fellow dad will be able to tell whether the food was grilled by an apron-less dad.

click!
click!

66. *A dad must give his grill tongs a couple of test clicks before using them. A dad is a grill artist, and his tongs are his paintbrush.*

DAD AND KIDS

· QUALITY TIME ·

01. Any dad who calls time with his kid "babysitting" is in violation of Dad Law. Spending time with your kid is called parenting.

02. When a child shows a dad a drawing, a dad will respond with praise, regardless of the actual quality of the piece. It's the thought that counts, and not the fact that the kid drew you as a complete circle and hurt your pride. You don't have five eyeballs and a tail either, but that's beside the point.

03. A dad will treasure any/all handmade crafts given to him as gifts from his child. Yes, this means he will wear a macaroni necklace from time to time, and he will do it with pride.

04. A dad will not lose his cool about glitter getting all over the house after the kids do crafts. Sure, he'll be finding it on himself for years, and it will probably affect the resale value of his home when glitter is permanently embedded in the carpet, but the important thing is that the kids expressed themselves creatively.

05. A dad will do his best to attend as many of the following as possible:

    a. school performances

    b. parent-teacher conferences

    c. sports practices/games

    d. musical performances

    e. father/daughter or father/son events

· NICKNAMES ·

06. Approved nicknames for kids include but are not limited to:

    a. Sport

    b. Bud/Buddy

    c. Pal

    d. Dude

    e. Little dude

    f. Big dude

    g. My dude

    h. Kiddo

    i. Champ

    j. My man

    k. Buckaroo

    l. Princess

07. A dad with only one child will refer to them as "my favorite child." A dad must never have a "favorite" child except under the aforementioned circumstance.

08. A dad will jokingly refer to the firstborn child as the "guinea pig" he practiced his parenting on.

• BABIES AND TODDLERS •

09. A dad of a baby, toddler, or small child will toss the child up in the air as high as possible and then catch them. He will not be swayed by the nervousness of his spouse, bystanders, or passersby.

10. A dad seeing a baby that is swaddled will compare the child to a burrito.

11. A dad holding someone else's baby will do so gently, but he is permitted to carry his own baby casually in a football hold.

12. If a baby hands a dad a toy phone, he will stop what he's doing and take the call: "Hello . . . What??? That's crazy! . . . Yeah? You need to talk to the boss? Sure thing . . . Here. It's for you."

13. Every time a dad picks up his toddler, he will comment, "Man, you're getting big!"

14. When a dad smells a dirty diaper, he will do one of the following:

    a. state, "It wasn't me!"

    b. say, "Uh-oh, someone needs a diaper change. Is it you?" to an older kid or fellow adult as a joke

· BEDTIME ROUTINES ·

15. A dad reading a bedtime story will do silly voices for different characters. He will be required to replicate these voices every night in exactly the same way until the child loses interest.

16. A dad asked to read a bedtime story that is particularly long is permitted to skip large chunks of text or even entire pages as long as the kid doesn't notice. Skipping the middle of *One Fish, Two Fish, Red Fish, Blue Fish* never harmed anyone's reading comprehension skills.

17. A dad will check for monsters whenever asked by his kid. He will be sure to confirm that there are no monsters in the following places:

    a. under the bed

    b. in any/all closets

    c. near any creepy shadows/shapes in the dark

18. When putting a child to bed, a dad will use one or more of the following statements to signify the end of his parenting shift:
    a. "Get some sleep, we got a big day tomorrow."
    b. "Don't let the bedbugs bite."
    c. "See you bright and early."
    d. "Sleep good, bud."
    e. "OK, lights out."
    f. "See you in the morning." (He'll probably see the kid in five minutes, when they get out of bed for a glass of water.)

· PLAYTIME ·

19. If his child asks him to play, a dad will play according to their wishes regardless of how "manly" or "tough" he considers himself to be. Being a good dad is the "manliest" thing a man can do. This includes enthusiastic involvement in:
    a. tea parties
    b. dress-up
    c. dance parties
    d. playing princesses
    e. painting fingernails
    f. playing dolls in any form
    g. doing crafts

19.   **h.** making/wearing friendship bracelets
(cont.)   **i.** listening to (or loudly singing along to) music he would otherwise not choose (e.g., the *Frozen* soundtrack)

20. A dad given imaginary food from a kid's play kitchen will insist it is the best thing he has ever tasted.

21. After getting down on the floor to play with a young child for a short amount of time, a dad will make one of the following statements or sounds as he's trying to get up:
- **a.** "I'm getting too old for this."
- **b.** "One of these days I'm not going to be able to get back up."
- **c.** "I'm not as young as I used to be."
- **d.** "Give your old man a push."
- **e.** "Guess I'm just gonna live here on the ground now."
- **f.** *various swear words*
- **g.** *joints popping*
- **h.** *extended grunt*

22. A dad will use his child as an excuse to buy all the toys he secretly wants to play with himself. He is now free to buy as many LEGO sets as he wants without judgment: "It's for the kids!" A dad laughs in the face of the upper age limit on toy packaging.

23. It is a dad's responsibility to regularly pretend to be a monster and chase happily screaming children around the house.

    a. He may choose from a tickle monster, dad monster, tiger, dragon, lion, etc.

    b. He will jump out without warning to surprise the kids.

    c. The sounds he will make include one or more of the following:

        i. "*Rarrr!*"

        ii. "I'm gonna get ya!"

        iii. "Oh no, I'm turning into (insert chosen monster or animal name)!"

        iv. "You better run!"

24. A dad is responsible for carrying his kids in various silly ways just for fun, including but not limited to:

    a. piggyback rides

    b. horsey rides

    c. "airplane" rides

    d. hanging them upside down "by their toes"

    e. fireman's carry (with optional spinning)

    f. hanging off his bicep like he's Superman

25. If asked (and sometimes, without being asked) a dad will help his kid build a blanket fort, which he will secretly enjoy as much as the child. Forts are awesome. Adults don't get enough forts in their lives.

· CLASSIC LINES ·

26. A dad will tell a kid, "I've forgotten more than you know."

27. If a kid asks, "Where are we going?" a dad will respond, "Going crazy."

28. A dad observing a kid who can't sit still will ask if they have "ants in (their) pants."

29. In the event that a child refuses to get up when asked, a dad must ask the child, "Are your legs broken?"

30. If a kid doesn't know one ultra-specific fact, a dad will tease them by asking, "What do they teach you in school?!"

31. If a dad doesn't know how to answer or explain something to his kid, he will default to one of the following responses:
  a. "You'll understand when you're older."
  b. "Ask your mother."
  c. "We'll talk about it later."
  d. "Good question!" followed by a distraction, subject change, or filibuster.
  e. "It's one of life's great mysteries."
  f. "What do *you* think?" Experienced dads can spin this to seem like a teachable moment using the Socratic method and not like a way to get out of answering the question.

32. When a kid does something well, a dad will tell everyone in the vicinity one of the following:
    a. "The apple doesn't fall far from the tree."
    b. "He takes after his old man."
    c. "She's a chip off the old block."
    d. "She gets that from me."
    e. "He's the spitting image of his old man."

33. When a kid does something bad, a dad will tell everyone in the vicinity one of the following:
    a. "That must be from his mother's side."
    b. "She doesn't get that from me."

34. If a dad observes a kid doing something good, he will mark the occasion by stating:
    a. "You done good, kid."
    b. "Who are you and what have you done with my kid?"
    c. "You made your old man proud."

35. If a dad encounters a child with a cool item (including but not limited to: a race car bed, a Power Wheels vehicle, or Super Mario pajamas), a dad must ask, "Hey, does that come in my size?!"
    a. Alternatively, a dad can pretend he wishes to steal the desired item, and although this runs the risk of upsetting the child, many dads still choose this method.

36. When his children are stressing him out, a dad will tell them that they are giving him gray hair. In the case of a bald dad, he may also blame them for the loss of his hair.

37. After performing a seemingly insignificant task (e.g., passing the salt), a dad has the option to remark, "Don't say I never did anything for you."

· INJURIES ·

38. When kids are being wild, a dad will inform them, "It's all fun and games until someone gets hurt." He will reiterate that he said this after one of the children does, in fact, get hurt.

39. If a kid has injured themselves, a dad will ensure that the child is all right before laughing. Even if it was hilarious, as kid injuries often are, he can't laugh until he confirms no permanent damage is done. If a child is particularly sensitive, a dad will hold his laughter until a later time when he's retelling the story.

40. When a kid gets hurt in front of a group of people, non-dads will audibly gasp or react dramatically. Dads know better. Dads will play it cool, knowing that kids will usually brush off any injuries that don't get a reaction.

41. Upon inspection of a small injury to their child (such as an inconsequential scratch or scrape), the required dad response is, "Looks like we'll have to amputate." This will have the effect of either entertaining the child and making them laugh as a distraction from the injury, or in rare cases, this will have the undesired result of making the child scream in terror. It's a gamble that dads are willing to take.

42. If a child is very upset about an insignificant injury or offense, a dad may try to console them by saying one of the following:
    a. "I think you'll live."
    b. "Walk it off."
    c. "Rub some dirt on it."

43. If a kid stubs their toe, a dad will say, "We better call a toe truck."

44. If a kid says, "It hurts when I do this (insert random particular movement)," a dad will offer very helpful advice: "Then don't do that."

45. A dad consoling an injured child will recount the time he did the same thing as a kid but ended up needing eleven stitches.

46. A dad will tell a kid with a significant injury that it will make a cool story one day, and maybe it will leave a cool scar. After all, chicks dig scars.

47. A dad will always place a Band-Aid on an "owie" if the child asks, regardless of whether the injury is real or imagined. He will also permit the child to put Band-Aids on him, or on a favorite teddy bear.

48. A dad placing a Band-Aid may refer to himself as "Dr. Dad," despite having little to no medical training.

49. A dad asked to kiss an owie will kiss it to make it feel better. No questions asked. Dad kisses are the only known panacea.

· RULES AND REGULATIONS ·

50. When a child has committed an offense, regardless of severity, a dad will respond by stating on the record, "I'm not mad; I'm just disappointed."

51. If a child is misbehaving, a dad will use the "I'm going to count to three" method.
    a. He is not required to know what will happen when he gets to three.

51.   **b.** He is permitted to stretch out "two" into increasingly
(cont.)   smaller increments to prevent reaching three (i.e.,
two and three-fourths . . .).

52.   If a kid is not listening to him, a dad will always say, "I'm not going to tell you again," before telling them again.

53.   If a kid tries to blame a sibling for a fight, a dad will be forced to respond with one of the following:
     a. "I don't care who started it—I'm finishing it."
     b. "It takes two to tango."
     c. "You're the older kid, so you need to set the example."
     d. "Learn to turn the other cheek."

54.   A dad who does not want to hear back talk will say one of the following:
     a. "No ifs, ands, or buts about it."
     b. "You get what you get and you don't throw a fit."
He will probably still get back talk, but at least he tried.

55.   If a kid is resisting instructions, a dad will say, "I'm not asking. I'm telling."

56.   If a member of the family breaks something (intentionally or unintentionally), a dad will declare, "This is why we can't have nice things."

57. If it's too loud in the house, a dad will say:

    a. "I can't hear myself think."

    b. "Put a sock in it."

    c. "Take it down about five notches, wouldja?"

    d. *yelling* *"Stop yelling!"*

58. *If a member of the family is being unruly and/or has left a door open when going outside, a dad will ask if they were raised in a barn. Only a barn-raised wildling would do such a thing.*

59. If a kid asks to do something they aren't usually allowed to do, a dad will ask, "What did your mom say?"

60. In response to any spill, a dad will not get angry but will calmly say:

    a. "No use crying over spilled milk."

    b. "Hand me those paper towels over there, wouldja?"

61. A dad setting a curfew will say, "Nothing good happens after midnight."

62. If a child questions why they must do something, a dad will respond, "Because I said so." This is the closing statement to any conversation. Amendments and addendums are strictly prohibited.

· SOCIAL INTERACTIONS ·

63. If a kid has a friend over, a dad will do one or more of the following:
    a. call the friend by the wrong name (intentionally or unintentionally)
    b. make the friend laugh so he can tell his own kid, "See, I told you I'm funny!"
    c. try to win the friend over by being the "fun" dad
    d. give the friend a nickname like "J-man"
    e. say, "You can pick your friend and you can pick your nose, but you can't pick your friend's nose."
    f. tell the friend she's part of the family now, so she better make herself at home

64. If a dad sees his child with a friend, he will refer to them as "double trouble." (This term will also be used to describe twins.)

65. If a dad observes kids groaning or being grossed out by him kissing his spouse, he will do it more dramatically, often with a dip to really sell it. He knows that one day they will remember how in love their parents were. One day, it won't seem gross at all. (But it is not this day.)

66. Given an opportunity, and sometimes completely unprompted, a dad will brag about his children. If his kids are within earshot and he can make them blush, all the better.

67. If a kid says, "Dad, you're embarrassing me!" a dad will respond by saying, "That's my job."

DAD AND TECHNOLOGY

· ADJUSTING TO MODERN TECHNOLOGY ·

01. If a modern product breaks for any reason whatsoever, a dad will always comment, "They don't make 'em like they used to."

02. A dad will have a simultaneous fascination with and mistrust of all new technologies he encounters. He will want to learn how they work but also can't stop himself from saying that machines are coming for all our jobs. When frustrated or impressed by new technology, some dads will simply mumble an ominous, "Skynet . . ."

03. *A dad will hang on to any/all cords from all electronics, even outdated ones. Just in case.*

04. A dad will tell kids how lucky they are to have electronics on long road trips, and how he used to have to just watch the scenery pass by for ten hours straight. (He will secretly be very relieved that they have these electronics, for his own sanity and ease of travel.)

05. A dad will be sure to educate his kids on other technology they have not experienced in their short lives, including but not limited to:
   a. records/record players/vinyl
   b. tapes/tape decks (including VHS)
   c. Atari/Pong/vintage gaming
   d. overhead projectors in classrooms
   e. the virtues of the Walkman
   f. the boom box he was never cool enough for
   g. old Nintendo game cartridges and how you blew on them if they weren't working

· INTERNET ·

06. A dad will always keep the Wi-Fi password written down on a scrap of paper in the junk drawer.

07. The Wi-Fi password will only be given to people deemed worthy by dad and may be withheld from those he feels haven't earned it. A dad giveth Wi-Fi and a dad taketh away Wi-Fi.

08. A dad is always responsible for resetting the router when the wireless isn't working. No one else can do it, apparently.

09. If he has discovered a funny internet video, a dad will insist that people watch it, often blissfully unaware that the video is three years old and everyone has already seen it.

10. When showing a person a funny internet video, a dad will:
   a. watch their face intently
   b. say, "Wait, this is the funny part, coming up."
   c. laugh loudly as if it's his first time seeing it
   d. ask if you liked it and appear disappointed if your response is not given with enough enthusiasm

11. Whenever possible, a dad will tell his kids about the days before the internet. He may also mention the lost art of "dial-up" or "AOL instant messaging."

· SOCIAL MEDIA ·

12. A dad will approach all forms of social media with suspicion and will have a general dislike for newer platforms. He may make a joke out of what he believes to be a new platform's primary use, for example: "Why is everyone on TikTok dancing?" However, a dad may enjoy Facebook or Instagram for the purposes of:

12.
(cont.)
   a. sharing and liking photos of his kids
   b. posting photos of his most recent home improvement and/or woodworking projects
   c. making and sharing dad jokes

13. A dad will upload the same unflattering Facebook profile photo at least eleven times in an attempt to get it to work, not realizing that it did work. (Every time.)

· EMAIL ·

14. A dad will complain about all the spam emails he receives. He doesn't remember signing up for any of them.

15. A dad will sign every email he sends, be it business or personal, with his full name.
   a. It will not be an auto signature. It's typed out by dad each time.
   b. He will use his first and last names, even when corresponding with his own kids.
   c. He may add "Dad" in parentheses after the full name if he prefers.
   d. A middle initial may be added in formal correspondence, to sound fancy.

16. A dad referring to the postal service will call it "snail mail." This is opposed to electronic mail, or "email" as the kids call it.
    a. A dad will have a friendly relationship with the mail carrier.
    b. A dad will avoid the post office if possible and complain about the lines at the post office if forced to go.
    c. A dad will always buy more stamps. Preferably Forever stamps, which, he will explain to those around him, are good forever.
    d. A dad will complain about the wasteful amounts of junk mail clogging his mailbox. How did they get his address anyway?

17. Whenever possible, a dad will buy a Bluetooth-enabled device. Bluetooth and dads go together like peanut butter and jelly.

· PHONES ·

18. A dad will tell his kids epic tales from the days before smartphones, including but not limited to:
    a. the days of "landlines"
    b. the size/model of the first cell phone they had
    c. the virtues of the flip phone

18.   **d.**   the invincible nature of the Nokia phone
(cont.)   **e.**   the fact that it used to take enormous computers (the size of an entire room) to do the work of that phone that sits in your pocket

19.   A dad will refer to a phone's battery level as "juice."

20.   A dad will never let his cell phone battery level (juice) dip below 50 percent without charging it.

21.   A dad answering his phone will use one of the following phrases:
   a.   "Yellllllllow."
   b.   "You got (dad's name)."
   c.   "(Dad's name) speaking, who is this?"

22.   When leaving a voicemail, a dad will:
   a.   open with, "It's Dad."
   b.   close with, "Give us a call."

23.   A dad leaving a voicemail for someone who called him first will say, "Looks like we're playing phone tag." Dads hate playing phone tag but love calling it that.

24. A dad will write short and succinct text messages whenever possible. A simple "OK" is always an acceptable text response from a dad, regardless of the length or urgency of the other texter's previous message.

25. If a text back is not received in the desired window of time, a dad will call to see if the person received the text.

26. A dad will constantly remind his kids of the very real dangers of texting and driving.

27. Dads are required to hold their phone at arm's length and tilt their head down while reading a text.

28. A dad who finds himself in a group text will do one or more of the following:
    a. complain about all the texts and ask, "Don't you have jobs?"
    b. join in the conversation sporadically with well-intentioned but occasionally awkward texts
    c. rain down dad jokes on the chat with no mercy

29. A dad watching a video on his phone in public will do so with the volume on max and no concern for those around him. He's blissfully unaware that this is simply not done in civilized non-dad society.

· FRUSTRATIONS ·

30. A dad experiencing frustration with the printer is permitted to swear at it.

    a. When the frustration has died down, a dad may sarcastically say, "I love this printer. I swear by it."

31. If a dad witnesses a technological issue while out in public (e.g., a problem with the register or card reader while checking out at the grocery store), he will state, "It's amazing we ever survived before computers."

32. A dad attempting to help someone with a technological problem of any kind will ask one or more of the following:

    a. "Is it plugged in?"

    b. "Have you tried turning it off and back on again?"

    c. "Can you jiggle the wires?"

Any technological issue that doesn't respond to these methods is beyond a typical dad's scope and abilities.

33. A dad who is proficient with computers or has been trained in any technology will become the IT consultant for every immediate and extended family member, as well as all neighbors, friends, and acquaintances. Even if he doesn't want to do it, he will be setting up a lot of iPads and troubleshooting every technological problem for the rest of eternity.

· TELEVISION ·

34. A dad will refer to the TV remote as "the clicker."

35. On the weekly occasion that the family cannot find the clicker, a dad will ask everyone in the room if they are sitting on it. However, if someone asks the same question of him, he will state that he "would be able to feel it if he was sitting on it."

36. A dad watching TV for any amount of time will comment that there are too many dang commercials.

37. A dad will complain about the volume of the commercials in comparison to the volume of the show he is watching.

SECTION VIII

DAD FASHION

· FOOTWEAR ·

01. A dad will rock a white sneaker.
   a. He may choose from New Balance or Nike Air Monarchs.
   b. He will purchase them on sale, never full price.
   c. If one pair is dirty or worn out, he will buy an identical pair as a replacement or spare.
   d. A clean pair of sneakers (still recognizable as white, not stained green from mowing the lawn) also counts as a dress shoe.
   e. A dad will have one pair of sneakers designated for yard work and mowing only. The level of dirt/grass stains on these sneakers will be a point of pride for him. You can tell how many years a man has been a dad by measuring the grass stains on his sneakers.

02. A dad will refer to new shoes as "new kicks."

03. A dad trying on new shoes will say, "Let me take 'em for a test-drive," and power walk around the store.

04. If a dad finds a particular type of plain sock that he likes, he must purchase this sock in bulk quantities. Good socks don't come around every day. You have to make the most of them.

05. A dad is permitted to own and wear a pair of Crocs. If anyone makes fun of him, he will concede that they are ugly but insist, "They're comfortable." Comfort is a dad's top fashion priority.

· PANTS AND SHORTS ·

06. Given a choice of shorts, a dad will always choose cargo shorts. You never know when a bit of cargo will come your way.

07. Cargo shorts are seasonally appropriate year-round. If a spouse states that it is not cargo shorts weather, a dad will educate them on Dad Law, which gives him permission.

08. A dad is the only person who can pull off pants that unzip into shorts. He will use these to mark the passing of the seasons by unzipping them when the temperature gets higher than 55 degrees.

09. If his cargo shorts are in the laundry, a dad will wear basketball shorts, despite rarely intending to play basketball. He'll be ready should a pickup game (or a nap) present itself.

10. A dad noticing jeans with holes in them is required to inform the wearer that he hopes they didn't pay full price for those.

· BELTS ·

11. A dad needs only two belts: a black one and a brown one. These two belts will last him the entirety of his life.

12. If a dad encounters a young man without a belt, he will tell him to wear a belt so his pants don't fall down. It doesn't matter the young man's age. Toddlers can wear belts too. Your Pull-Ups are showing. It's embarrassing.

13. A dad will clip his phone to his belt whenever possible and convenient.

· FORMAL ATTIRE ·

14. A dad who is required to attend a formal or semiformal occasion will ask if a "nice pair of jeans" will suffice. They usually will, in his opinion.

15. A dad will wear khakis and a tucked-in shirt when the attire is designated as "business casual." The shirt may be either a polo or button-up.

16.   If a dad sees a friend unusually dressed up, he will tease, "Nice suit. Got a court date?"

17.   A dad complimenting another dad's tie will call it "snazzy."

18.   A dad seeing his family dressed up will approvingly say they "clean up all right." This compliment borders on gushing.

19.   A dad will put off buying a new suit because they're so expensive and the old one "still fits." The actual fit of the suit is irrelevant as long as the dad can physically get it on his body.

20.   A dad seeing someone wearing something he wouldn't wear will ask them if they "lost a bet."

21.   A dad who receives a free T-shirt from work will wear it regularly for fifteen years, at minimum.

22.   A dad will always carry a pen in his pocket and will remind those around him how important it is to "keep a pen on ya." In the event that someone needs a pen, a dad will be the first to proudly pull his out.

· VACATION ATTIRE ·

23. A dad on vacation is permitted to wear any/all of the following, even if they are not in his usual wardrobe rotation (and let's hope they aren't):

   a. a loud Hawaiian shirt he's been saving for just such an occasion

   b. a fanny pack

   c. sandals, inexplicably paired with socks

   d. a hat with the vacation city's name on it

   e. a T-shirt that says, "I went to _____ and all I got was this lousy T-shirt."

   f. an enormous camera, even though everyone just uses their phones now

   g. jean shorts (to be efficiently referred to as "jorts")

   h. khaki shorts and shirt, because apparently he's the Crocodile Hunter now?

   i. surfer apparel e.g., a T-shirt with the hang loose symbol, even though a dad has never hung loose)

· OUTERWEAR AND ACCESSORIES ·

24. The highest compliment a dad can pay a jacket is to say, "It keeps the wind off ya." You definitely wouldn't want the wind on ya, now would ya?

25. A dad who is uncomfortable with his receding hairline will wear baseball caps when possible. A dad who is comfortable with his receding hairline may decide to just shave it all off. Both are acceptable. All dad hairlines are beautiful.

26. A dad who wears transition lenses will have no shame about them. You can laugh and make fun of him behind his back—everyone does—but they are extremely convenient and a dad never apologizes for choosing convenience.

27. A dad who chooses to wear flip-up shades on his glasses is not to be trifled with. That man is fearless.

28. If a dad is wearing aviator sunglasses or in close proximity to someone wearing aviator sunglasses, he is required to bring up *Top Gun*. He is always Maverick, never Goose.

29. When frustrated, a dad will take off his glasses and rub the bridge of his nose where they rest. If a dad just removed his glasses to rub his face, steer clear. He's barely holding it together.

Absolutely not …

30.   *Dads don't let fellow dads wear fedoras.*

31.   A dad is permitted to keep and wear the same ski jacket for every cold weather occasion for years to come. If he's been skiing in the last decade or two, he may leave the lift ticket still attached as a badge of honor.

· GROOMING ·

32.   A dad will refer to his gray hair as "salt and pepper" and compare himself to George Clooney. It may be the only trait he shares with George Clooney, but it's something.

33.   A dad will refer to his physique, whatever it may be, as a "dad bod." Dad bods are to be celebrated.

34.   All dads have considered what they would look like with a Tom Selleck mustache. All of them. They would all look incredible, by the way.

35. A dad who *can* grow a beard *will* grow a beard at some point, just to show he can.

36. If a dad is shaving off his beard, he will first shave it into a variety of humorous facial-hair styles to take photos and/or show his family to make them laugh (e.g., tiny mustache, goatee, etc.).

37. A dad shaving over the sink will try to remember to clean out all the little stubble hairs, but he's not perfect, OK?

38. A dad will only use a deodorant with an illustration of an old-timey ship on the label, a ridiculous name such as "Grizzly Bear Facepunch," or both.

39. A dad will wear cologne on special occasions but will prefer piney type smells to flowery smells. It is unclear why trees are acceptable to him but not other plants.

· FAMILY CLOTHING ·

40. A dad dressing his baby is not confined to society's rules of fashion or "matching." If it looks like it's around the right size, it will go on the baby. It's day care, not a fashion show.

41. A dad will refer to the color of an article of clothing only by its simplest name (e.g., blue) and will have little ability to distinguish between varied shades (e.g., periwinkle, navy, teal).

42. A dad will complain about how much space his spouse takes up in the closet and will jokingly be upset if he finds an item of his spouse's clothing has encroached upon his closet territory. (He doesn't actually mind; he just likes to take any opportunity to tease his spouse and he doesn't have much to work with.)

43. A dad will put clothes in the washing machine regardless of tags specifying "hand wash only" or "dry clean only." These instructions do not apply to dads.

DAD LANGUAGE AND TERMINOLOGY

· GOVERNING LANGUAGE PRINCIPLES ·

01. If there is a chance to use a pun, a dad will take it. It is his "respunsibility."

02. A dad may state, "No pun intended," when, in fact, the pun was intended. Very intended. He just wants to draw the listener's attention to what a good pun it was.

03. A dad will reuse a particular joke or anecdote for years to come if it got a laugh the first time. He will expect the same laugh to happen each subsequent time and will be baffled as to why his family is rolling their eyes now.

04. A dad will laugh at his own joke if it was particularly amusing. Which it probably was. These guys just don't appreciate a well-crafted zinger.

05. If a dad has made several jokes in a row and no one has laughed or acknowledged him, he will grab the closest object and tap it like a microphone while asking, "Is this thing on?" An air microphone can be used in dire circumstances.

06. A dad who steals the punch line of another dad and receives the laughs rightly deserved by the first dad will be found in violation of Dad Law. This is a treasonous dad crime.

07. A dad who has heard a new slang term is required to purposefully misuse or overuse this term with the intention of embarrassing his children in front of their friends.

· STORYTELLING AND NARRATIVES ·

08. A dad telling a story will open with, "So there I was, minding my own business . . ." It is important that you know he was just minding his own business. Like always.

09. A dad will exaggerate his stories by 3 percent with each year that passes. It's unclear whether he does this consciously or subconsciously, but at some point he will seem to truly believe the embellished stories.

10. A dad can speak a thousand words with a single pair of finger guns.

· CLEVER COMEBACKS ·

11. A dad's required response to the word "Hey" is "Hay is for horses."

12.   If a child states that he or she is hungry, a dad will respond, "Hi, Hungry. I'm Dad."

13.   If a kid says, "I'm thirsty," a dad will respond, "I'm Friday. Come over Saturday and we'll have a Sundae."

14.   If a kid says, "I have a question," a dad will respond, "I have an answer."

15.   If someone says, "See you later, alligator," a dad will respond, "After a while, crocodile."

16.   If someone asks a dad, "Guess what?" he will respond, "Chicken butt."

17.   If someone asks a dad if he's "all right," he will respond, "No, I'm half left."

18.   If someone says, "I was thinking . . . ," a dad will state, "I thought I smelled smoke!"

19.   If a child asks if they can do something, a dad will respond, "I don't know, *can* you?" The intent is either to teach the child about the grammatical differences between "can" and "may" or just to be obnoxious.

20. If there is an obvious answer to a question, a dad must say, "I'll give you three guesses." The person is not actually expected to guess.

· IN A HURRY ·

21. In the event that something a dad is doing is taking longer than expected, said dad is required to state, "You can't rush art."

22. If a dad wants something done quickly, he will say one or more (or sometimes all) of the following:
  a. "C'mon, we're burning daylight."
  b. "Chop chop."
  c. "Hop to it."
  d. "Shake a leg."
  e. "Get a move on."
  f. "Hustle."
  g. "Tick tock."
  h. *humming the Jeopardy! theme song*
  i. "Step on it."
  j. "Snap to it."
  k. "Look alive."
  l. "Make it snappy."
  m. "Time is money."
  n. "What are you waiting for? An engraved invitation?"

23. A dad will describe the process of getting his family to complete a task as being "like herding cats."

24. A dad who wants to ask his family for more patience will tell them:
    a. "Hold your horses."
    b. "Cool your jets."
    c. "Take a chill pill."
    d. "Just sit tight."
    e. "Good things come to those who wait."
    f. "Patience is a virtue."

25. A dad who is relieved that something is finally done will say one of the following:
    a. "About time."
    b. "Took you long enough."
    c. "I never thought I'd see the day."
    d. "Just in the nick of time."

· NICKNAMES ·

26. A dad may create a nickname for a male individual at any time. This nickname cannot be revoked once declared and will be one of the following:
    a. The person's first name followed by "-meister"
    b. Brother

26.
(cont.)
   c. Chief
   d. Boss
   e. Hoss
   f. Tough guy
   g. Big guy (reserved for small people)
   h. Shortie (reserved for tall people)

27. A dad will refer to his spouse as one or more of the following:

   a. the wife
   b. my better half
   c. the missus
   d. the old ball and chain (This is permitted only if the dad is saying it affectionately but actually loves his spouse. It is not permitted as an actual slight.)

· NEGATIVE LANGUAGE ·

28. A dad will use creative language to hint at profound dislike for someone without coming right out and saying it. He may use one or more of the following phrases to describe someone he dislikes:

   a. "He's not playing with a full deck."
   b. "He's not the sharpest tool in the shed."
   c. "He's a few sandwiches short of a picnic."
   d. "He's all hat and no cattle."

28.
(cont.)

    e. "The lights are on but nobody's home."

    f. "I only trust him about as far as I can throw him."

    g. "He's a real piece of work."

29. A dad will describe someone in a noticeably bad mood as having one or more of the following:

    a. a bee in their bonnet

    b. a chip on their shoulder

    c. their underwear in a twist

30. A dad who is feeling angry or upset will express that he's:

    a. about to blow:

        i. his top

        ii. a gasket

        iii. a fuse

    b. ready to fly off the handle

    c. fit to be tied

    d. pretty steamed

    e. had it up to here

    f. at the end of his rope

    g. at his wit's end

31. A dad who is annoyed by something in particular will say, "That really gets my goat."

32. A dad is permitted to swear in extreme circumstances (or in the car; see Section III, Article 14) but will mostly try to stick to softened-down swears including but not limited to:

    a. heck

    b. sonofa

    c. dang it

    d. well, shoot

33. A dad wishing to reduce his swearing may employ the use of a swear jar. A dad may proclaim the funds be used for ice cream. One night, when he's craving ice cream, a bold dad will let out a string of (relatively innocent) curses so the family can get ice cream (and to make the kids laugh).

34. A dad encountering a problem will say, "Houston, we have a problem." An accompanying staticky-type sound, as if it's coming in over the speakers from space, is recommended but not required.

35. A dad who means "No, absolutely not, never" may use one of the following phrases as a substitute:

    a. "When pigs fly."

    b. "That'll be a cold day in hell."

    c. "Over my dead body."

    d. "We'll see."

    e. "I'll think about it."

36. A dad observing someone doing something in a comically poor way will tell them, "Don't quit your day job." This is especially funny if it's a kid with no day job.

· POSITIVE LANGUAGE ·

37. An especially pleased dad may state, "I owe ya one," in place of "Thank you."

38. Upon being thanked, a dad will respond with one of the following approved statements:
   a. "You betcha."
   b. "No problemo."

39. A dad describing two people who get along well will say they:
   a. get on like a house on fire
   b. are as thick as thieves
   c. get on like gangbusters

40. A dad will use one or more of the following phrases to describe someone he likes:
   a. "He's sharp as a tack."
   b. "That's my guy/boy/man/dude/girl."
   c. "That's one tough cookie."

41. A dad observing someone doing something strenuous or stupid will muse, "Oh, to be young again."

42. If a dad is very confident in something, he will say, "You can bet the farm on it." A dad will use this expression sparingly though, because you can't just go betting the farm on any old thing.

43. A dad who is excited to show you something may preface it with:
    a. "Feast your eyes on this!"
    b. "Take a gander."
    c. "I'm about to knock your socks off."
    d. *drumroll sound*

44. If he senses low morale in his family, a dad will attempt to cheer them up through pep talks and encouragement. He will refer to this as "rallying the troops."

45. If someone tries to tease a dad, he will tell them you can't kid a kidder.

46. If a dad sees someone stumble while walking, he will very helpfully say one of the following:
    a. "Have a nice trip; see you next fall."
    b. "First day on the new legs?"

47. A dad hearing surprising news will respond with one of the following phrases:
    a. "No kidding?"
    b. "Are you pullin' my leg?"
    c. "I'll be darned."
    d. "Shut the front door."
    e. "Well, I'll be a monkey's uncle."

48. If a kid asks when mom is going to be home, a dad will simply answer, "When she gets here." He's not wrong.

• DAD PHRASES •

49. A dad will constantly remind those around him that he wasn't born yesterday. Just in case you started thinking he was born yesterday, he wasn't. Additionally, he may have been born at night, but it wasn't last night.

50. A dad will always say "half a dozen," even though it is much faster to just say "six."

51. If a kid almost finished their chores, almost ate all their vegetables, or almost beat their dad in Mario Kart, the dad will say, "Almost only counts in horseshoes and hand grenades."

52.   If a dad overhears any poor sap make an accidental rhyme while speaking, it initiates code RHYME TIME. He will jump on the opportunity and say, "You're a poet and you didn't even know it."

53.   When trying to figure out the plan, a dad will ask, "What's the plan, Stan?" "Roseanne" may be used as a replacement for Stan. Failure to tag one of these on to "the plan" is a violation of Dad Law.

54.   If a dad requests that you "crack a window," he means to open the window just a little. He does not mean you should throw a baseball through it and shatter it. Just clearing that up.

55.   When trying to learn something new, a dad will jokingly say, "You can't teach an old dog new tricks." In truth, he very much hopes you can teach an old dog new tricks, but he's not sure yet.

· MEDICAL TERMINOLOGY ·

56.   A dad will likely resist going to the doctor, saying, "It's nothing." If it becomes clear that it's something, he will then insist he can tough it out. The best way to get a dad to go to the doctor is to lure him into the car by saying you're

56.
(cont.) going to the hardware store, then drive him to the doctor's office instead. He may be mad but it's for his own good, and maybe he can have a treat after.

57. A dad will always call his doctor "Doc." It is not meant as disrespect and is in fact a term of endearment.

58. A dad will always refer to getting surgery as "going under the knife." This is the most unpleasant way to phrase it, but dads can't help themselves.

59. A dad who is not feeling well will say he is:
    a. sick as a dog
    b. under the weather
    c. on his deathbed

60. A dad who is feeling better after being sick will refer to himself as one of the following:
    a. fit as a fiddle
    b. healthy as a horse
    c. back from the dead
    d. still kickin'

61. If a dad has an injury of any kind, he will say, "You should see the other guy!" There is no other guy.

62. A dad is permitted to cry. There is absolutely no shame in crying. However, a dad wishing to deflect attention from his crying will state one or more of the following as a diversion:

    a. "Who's cutting onions in here?"

    b. "I've got dust in my eye."

    c. "I'm not crying, you're crying."

(He may also comment with any of these phrases on the internet under a heartwarming video of a dog and duck who are friends.)

63. A dad who thinks someone is being crazy will ask them one of the following:

    a. "Are you off your gourd?"

    b. "Have you lost your marbles?" (One must always hold on to one's marbles.)

    c. "Are you off your rocker?"

    d. "Do you have a screw loose?"

64. A dad will describe someone he thinks is getting old to be "no spring chicken."

65. A dad will tease a friend who just had a vasectomy about "shootin' blanks."

66. A dad who has suffered a shock will say one of the
    following:
    a. "That scared the living daylights out of me."
    b. "I'm sh*ttin' bricks."
    c. "You gave me a heart attack."
    d. "You scared the bejeebers out of me!" ("The bejeebers"
       is a formal medical term.)

67. A dad will describe someone who frequently says
    embarrassing things as having "foot in mouth disease."
    He may have the condition himself, on occasion.

DADVICE AND CLICHÉS

· GIVING ADVICE ·

01. A dad will take any opportunity to give his kids advice. It's one of the most important parts of the whole fatherhood gig.

02. When giving advice, a dad will often preface it with one of the following:
   a. "Do as I say, not as I do."
   b. "I've been around the block a few times."
   c. "Let me show you a trick I learned in 'Nam," even if (especially if) he wasn't in 'Nam.
   d. "This isn't my first rodeo." All dads have extensive metaphorical rodeo experience.

03. As often as possible, a dad will incorporate a cliché or catchy phrase into the advice he gives. This will help the advice stick in the kids' minds. The more annoyed the kids seem by the repetition of the advice, the more likely they will remember it as adults. One day they may even find themselves telling their own kids all the classic dad advice they once rolled their eyes at.

04. A dad who doesn't have good advice or an answer will say, "We'll cross that bridge when we come to it."

05. A dad will say you don't have to take his advice, but don't come crying to him when things go south. (Of course, you can come crying to him later, but he'll tell you, "Told you so.")

· PRACTICAL ADVICE ·

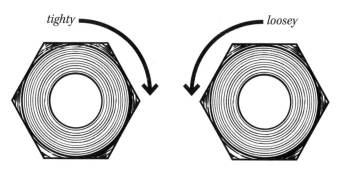

tighty   *loosey*

06. *A dad's most sacred advice is the old adage, "Righty tighty, lefty loosey."*

07. Regardless of the item, a dad will always recommend, "Hang on to that; it may come in handy someday." You'd be amazed how many things come in handy if you hoard them long enough.

08. In the event of a child becoming frustrated with a particular object, a dad must inform them, "It's a poor craftsman who blames his tools."

09. A dad will remind his family, "If it ain't broke, don't fix it."

10. A dad who has grown tired of answering questions will say, "Curiosity killed the cat."

11. A dad will advise you to make sure you don't put the cart before the horse. While a horse-led cart is a pretty sweet situation, a cart-led horse? An unmitigated disaster.

12. A dad will tell you to take any chance to "kill two birds with one stone." Killing just one bird with a stone is for amateurs.

13. A dad will remind a bored kid, "Only boring people get bored." If the kid is really that bored, a dad can find some chores for them to do.

14. Even if the kid is too young to follow the metaphor, a dad shouldn't resist sprinkling in some metaphor-rich adages, including but not limited to:

    a. "Make sure you aren't too busy fighting alligators to drain the swamp."

    b. "Don't throw out the baby with the bathwater."

    c. "There's more than one way to skin a cat."

When the toddler stares back blankly, the dad can move along. No further explanation necessary. They'll get it one day.

15. To teach preparedness, a dad must tell his child, "It's better to have it and not need it than need it and not have it." This is a convincing argument to take an umbrella even if there's only a slight chance of rain. If the kid doesn't take the umbrella and gets soaked, the dad will have stated this on the record and can remind them of that, forever.

· CLASSIC LIFE LESSONS ·

16. It is a dad's responsibility to remind the family that "life isn't fair."

17. A dad is required to ask his kid the age-old philosophical question, "If your friends jumped off a cliff, would you?"

18. A dad will preach that "where there's a will, there's a way."

19. A dad will remind his family that "if something's worth doing, it's worth doing right the first time."

20. A dad will encourage a kid to "give it the ol' college try" before giving up.

21. Whenever someone goes through something unpleasant, a dad will tell them one or more of the following:

    a. "It builds character."

    b. "It's a learning experience."

    c. "It will put hair on your chest."

DAD PRANKS AND TRICKERY

• TEASING KIDS •

01. A dad derives joy from teasing his kids whenever he can. It's one of the ways dads express affection and love—by being playful for a reaction. Also, it's hilarious.

02. Upon hearing police sirens, a dad will tell the nearest child, "Oh no! They're comin' for ya!"

03. When participating in a high five, a dad is required to initiate the traditional "down low, too slow" protocol (especially if the other party is unsuspecting). An advanced "in space, in your face" variation is permissible when done playfully.

04. A dad will perform the "got your nose!" illusion whenever the opportunity presents itself.

05. If a kid swallows a watermelon seed, a dad will say, "Oh no! You're going to grow a watermelon in your stomach!" (This may be adapted to other types of seeds as needed.)

06. When play-wrestling and/or roughhousing with a small child, a dad will pretend to be hurt and defeated by the kid's super strength. This is both funny and flattering to a kid who suddenly feels like a big shot and is only half sure dad's joking.

07. When a kid is hiding very obviously in plain sight, a dad will pretend to be perplexed and say, "I wonder where (name of kid) could be?!" He will wait until the child jumps out and will pretend to be scared.

08. A dad is required to send each/all of his kids on a "snipe hunt" at some point in his fatherhood career.

09. A dad may purposefully (gently) sit on a child and then say, "Oh, sorry, I didn't see you there!" He will use caution to ensure the kid is laughing and not crushed under his formidable dad bod.

10. A dad may tease a child by saying, "You're a good kid. I don't care what they say about you."

11. If a kid complains about their nose running, a dad must respond, "Well, you better catch it."

12. A dad, upon witnessing his child picking their nose, will ask one of the following important medical questions:
   a. "Diggin' for gold?"
   b. "Did you pick a winner?"

13. If a little kid asks, "Can you put my shoes on?" a dad will shrug and say, "OK, but I don't think they'll fit me."

14. If a dad observes a kid putting their shoes on the wrong feet, he will tease, "Looks like you got your feet on wrong!"

15. If a kid has an untied shoe, a dad will tell them he has "a flat tire."

· STRATEGIC TRICKERY ·

16. If a dad asks a kid to get ready to go and the child refuses, he will dramatically say, "OK, I guess we'll have to go without you!" He may have to start slowly moving toward the door if the child tries to call his bluff.

17. A dad will ask unsuspecting individuals, "Does it smell like updog in here?" This sets him up for the funniest line of all time. If it works, the dad will never let it go.

18. *A dad will seize any opportunity to ask someone to pull his finger. Then you know what comes next.*

19. After farting, a dad will do one of the following:
    a. act like a kid did it, to make them mad
    b. blame it on the dog, who can't deny it
    c. ask, "Did somebody step on a duck?"

20. When a child has a loose tooth, a dad will jokingly offer to pull it out for them with pliers, or by tying the tooth to a doorknob and slamming the door shut. The fear of this will often encourage a kid to just yank the tooth out themself.

21. A dad will tell a kid that if they don't stop making that goofy face it will get stuck like that. It is unclear whether this is a threat or a challenge.

22. If a child is in possession of a toy that makes obnoxious sounds, a dad will remove its batteries and tell the child that the toy must be broken.

· EYE ROLL-INDUCING SILLINESS ·

23. If a dad sees a photo of himself, he will ask, "Who's that handsome devil?"

24. If a dad encounters an individual wearing camouflage, he will say he's not able to see this person. Camouflage makes you literally invisible to dads.

25. If someone asks for a hand with something, a dad will clap. This is neither helpful nor funny to the person in need of assistance but is funny to the dad, which is the most important thing.

26. A dad finding himself in close proximity to a deck of playing cards will ask if anyone wants to play "Fifty-Two Card Pickup."

27. A dad will periodically toss the car keys to a very young child and say, "You're driving!" When the kid inevitably protests and says, "I'm only seven!" a dad will pretend he forgot that fact.

28. If someone returns to get something they forgot, a dad will tease:
   a. "Back already?"
   b. "Well, that was fast."
   c. "How was it?"

29. If someone shows a dad a photo of them with a zoo animal, a dad will ask, "Which one is you?"

30. A dad will do his best to perfect the "going down the stairs behind the couch" illusion. It is an art and requires both practice and natural athleticism.

31. A dad will pretend all the ladies were after him when he was younger. His goofy yearbook photo and retro video game collection beg to differ.

32. A dad will joke that his recent weight gain is "sympathy weight" to go along with his spouse's pregnancy, even though everyone knows there is no such thing as sympathy weight.

33. If someone asks a dad, "Can I get you anything else?" a dad will respond with, "Yeah, a million dollars."

34. A dad seeing a baby photo will say to the person in it, "You used to be so cute. What happened?" What a burn!

35. If a dad sees something that's clearly for someone else (such as a birthday cake or gift) he will pretend he thinks it's for him and say, "For me? You shouldn't have!"

36. A dad near an electrical device will pretend to be electrocuted by it if he feels he has the right audience for such a prank. (This is called "Pulling a Dr. Grant," in reference to the character by that name who pretends to be electrocuted by an inactive electric fence in *Jurassic Park*.)

37. A dad will try to look tough by putting out a candle by wetting his fingers and pinching the wick. This will impress no one, and may even hurt a little sometimes, but it must be done.

38. If someone asks a dad what time it is, he will not give the time but will instead respond with one of the following:
    a. "Time for you to get a watch."
    b. "It's two hairs past a freckle."
    c. "Why? You got a big date?"

39. A dad talking about someone will say, "Speak of the devil," if that person comes into the room. He may also say this even if he wasn't talking about the person, just to get under their skin.

· DISCLAIMER ·

40. After teasing or pranking, a dad will clarify that his intentions were good by stating one of the following on the record:
    a. "I'm just pullin' your leg."
    b. "I'm just yankin' your chain."
    c. "I'm just joshin' ya."
    d. "I'm just givin' you a hard time."

DAD OUTDOORS

01. It is rare to find a dad who doesn't enjoy the great outdoors in some capacity, as it is their natural habitat. Depending on the dad, preferred outdoor activities can range from intense mountain hikes to sleeping in a hammock under a tree in the backyard.

02. A dad will constantly tell his family to go outside and get some fresh air. House air is not fresh air. Too many fingers have been pulled in here.

03. A dad will tell his family that a little dirt never hurt anyone. In fact, it's good to get dirty! It builds your immune system. (This does not apply to dirt that's been tracked into the house, which is the greatest of evils.)

· WEATHER ·

04. If the temperature is 82 degrees Fahrenheit or higher, a dad will say one of the following to anyone he passes:
   a. "Hot enough for ya?"
   b. "It's a scorcher."
   c. "It's hotter than blazes."
   d. "It's not the heat that gets ya, it's the humidity."
   e. "At least it's a dry heat."

05. A dad will initiate and/or participate in at least one water fight per summer. This may include any of the following:

    a. spraying kids with a garden hose

    b. water balloons

    c. Super Soakers

While it may begin playfully, it always escalates with surprising intensity.

06. If a spouse is trying to stay dry or says, "Don't you dare!" to the dad during a water fight, he is required to proceed to soak them. There's no mercy in water fighting.

07. Upon hearing of an upcoming storm in the forecast, a dad will be sure to do one or more of the following:

    a. plan a grocery run to stock up on emergency supplies such as milk, batteries, and beer

    b. question the legitimacy of the forecast, voicing a distrust of whatever news organization reported it

    c. check the radar on his phone regularly to give everyone updates

    d. do that thing where he licks his finger and holds it in the air to judge wind direction, or whatever. It's pointless.

    e. watch the sky for clouds. If spotted, he may state:

        i. "I don't like the looks of those clouds."

        ii. "Storm's-a-brewin'." (Said quickly like one word.)

07.
(cont.)

    iii. "Looks like rain (or snow)."

    iv. "Batten down the hatches."

    v. "Better move the car into the garage."

08. In the event of an actual storm, a dad will look out the window and remark one or more of the following:

    a. "We needed this rain."

    b. "It's a doozy."

    c. "I knew it; my knee was acting up." (A dad's old injury acting up is always the most accurate predictor of meteorological conditions.)

    d. "Good thing we aren't out there."

    e. "It's raining cats and dogs."

    f. "We won't be needing to water the lawn today."

09. If he judges the storm to be of significant size, a dad will compare it to other notably large storms in his past (e.g., "Still not as bad as the blizzard of '94. Never seen anything like it.").

10. A dad will tell tales of his childhood, when he had to walk to school uphill, both ways, in the snow. No dad ever had anything easy in his childhood. Unlike these kids, who don't know how good they have it.

11. A dad will remind all members of his family to put on and zip up a coat before going outside. Even if you're only walking from the car into school, you need your coat or you'll get a chill.

12. A dad playing in the snow with his children will do one or more of the following winter dad activities:
    a. teach them proper snowman-building techniques
    b. show them how to catch snowflakes on their tongues
    c. have a snowball fight that gets a little too rough, accidentally
    d. try to trick them into shoveling the walk by pretending it's super fun, the ultimate ruse
    e. demonstrate a snow angel, although it will be an angel with a dad bod
    f. attempt to build a snow cave or fort and give up when it collapses

· CAMPING ·

13. A dad on a camping trip will:
    a. state that camping is "in tents." He may do this multiple times throughout the trip. Family members should try not to laugh the first time if they'd like to reduce recurrence.
    b. demonstrate how to light a campfire as if he's an expert

13.
(cont.)

 c. oversee the preparation of s'mores, including the correct procedure for the roasting of marshmallows. A toasted marshmallow should be golden brown and evenly cooked on all sides.

 d. struggle with the tent poles until he cusses under his breath

 e. tell a scary story with a flashlight under his face that is just a *bit* too scary to be age appropriate for all children involved

 f. identify the three types of trees he knows as if he knows all the types of trees in existence

 g. suddenly act like a mountain man and/or survival expert like Bear Grylls

 h. wonder out loud how long he could survive in the wild, even though everyone knows it wouldn't be long

14. A dad outside at night is required to point out well-known constellations like the Big Dipper and the North Star. These are likely the only things he can identify. Impressive though, right?

15. A dad who enjoys fishing will:

 a. constantly remind people he'd rather be fishing

 b. repeat the same story of the biggest fish he ever caught for years, until it becomes twisted into an exaggerated urban legend

16. A dad observing an incredible view at a beautiful location will remark, "Not a bad view, huh?"

17. A dad will take any chance to pull out his pocketknife to help with something. You rolled your eyes when he bought it, but look how it's coming in handy now.

18. A dad will attempt to identify poison ivy wherever he goes. Poison ivy is one of a dad's natural enemies, along with quicksand (which he's never encountered but has a deep-rooted fear of thanks to the movies he watched as a kid).

19. A dad will teach those around him on a hike everything he knows about snakes, which is usually only these two facts:
     a. "That's just a garter snake; he's harmless."
     b. the well-known "red and yellow, killed a fellow" rhyme about identifying poisonous snakes, although he can't quite remember how it goes now. Maybe it's red and yellow, *never* killed a fellow? Either way, probably best to avoid snakes.

20. A dad who claims to love trail mix really just likes to eat the M&M's out of it. They count as health food because it's trail mix.

21. A dad will always have bug spray on hand and will offer to spray anyone in his path. You don't want to be caught without it, not when it's this buggy out.

22. A dad encountering mosquitoes will say one or more of the following:
    a. "I'm being eaten alive."
    b. "Mosquitoes love me for some reason."
    c. "Did you know mosquitoes are the state bird of Minnesota?"

DAD AND HOME/YARD MAINTENANCE

· HOME IMPROVEMENT ·

01. If a dad has a no-swearing policy, this policy does not apply to home improvement projects. (Or driving; see Section III, Article 14.)

02. A dad hanging something on the wall must always hold it up and ask a member of the family if it looks level to them. Failure to confirm with the spouse that it looks level would be blatantly irresponsible.

03. Before use of a stud finder, a dad must point it at himself and state, "Found one." He is required to keep making the joke until someone acknowledges it.

04. A dad may describe a small measurement as "just a skosh."

05. A dad will keep a well-stocked supply of all of the following:
   a. every type of battery
   b. extension cords
   c. duct tape
   d. WD-40
   e. flashlights
   f. light bulbs

06. Upon completion of a home improvement project, a dad will do one or more of the following:

    a. fold his arms and admire it while declaring, "Not too shabby."

    b. brag that it took only three trips to the home improvement store

    c. brag that he did not have to call in any professionals (or, in dire circumstances, utilized fewer than three professionals)

    d. post about it on Facebook

07. A dad will remind those around him to change the furnace filter every six months, even if they have no idea where the furnace filter is or what it does.

08. A dad who owns a powerful flashlight will tell you how many lumens it is, for some reason.

09. A dad fixing something under the sink will ask his kid to hold the flashlight for him and will remind him to hold it steady.

10. Upon hearing any type of problem, a dad will state that he "has a guy for that." He will insist you take his guy's number. He's a great guy.

· SNOW REMOVAL ·

11. When encountering a neighbor shoveling snow, a dad will say, "Don't stop there; there's plenty at my house too."

12. A dad with a snowblower will derive great pleasure from the first snowblower run of the season. It is oddly satisfying.

13. A dad without a snowblower will say he needs to get himself a snowblower because shoveling is getting too hard on his back.

· FURNITURE ·

14. A dad (or group of dads) lifting something heavy will:
    a. issue a reminder to lift from your knees, not with your back
    b. state that the object is "not heavy, just awkward." This will be said even when the object is clearly heavy.

15. A dad will try not to complain if a family member wants to move furniture around "just to see how it looks." However, he will not move said furniture more than three times. This is getting ridiculous.

16. A dad shall not undertake the task of putting together a piece of IKEA furniture unless it is known that he is of sound mind, in a good mood, and his marriage is particularly strong. He will be putting all of these at risk once he starts trying to build that bookshelf. Unless you're going to compliment his progress or find that lost bolt, stay out of his way.

17. If a dad has extra bolts left over after building IKEA furniture and he's unsure where they should have been used, he will hide them and never speak of them again. No one needs to know.

· TOOLS ·

18. When using a power drill, a dad is required to rev it at least twice to ensure it's working, but mostly just because it sounds really cool. He may also hold the drill like a gun and recite his favorite '80s action hero's one-liner while loading the battery like a clip.

19. A dad revving a power tool will do his best to resist the urge to grunt like Tim Allen.

20. A dad will "measure twice, cut once." Measuring three times is acceptable, but never just once.

21. A dad can fix anything with duct tape. Anything. Unless it's something that needs to move, in which case WD-40 does the trick.

22. A dad who knows how to fix a few basic things will state, "If I can't fix it, it ain't broke."

23. A dad will call anything that breaks a "piece of junk." Even if he loved it just moments before.

24. A dad with a new power tool will refer to it as a "new toy."

25. A dad using a pressure washer shall not be interfered with under any circumstances. He is in a happy place.

26. A dad who keeps his tools in the garage will describe his time there as "tinkering" in the garage. This is a sacred time during which he is not to be disturbed.

27. A dad will keep his tools as organized as possible and say, "A place for everything and everything in its place."

28. A dad will not respond well to people borrowing his tools and not putting them back in the right spot. No, he will not like that at all.

29. Despite his diligence, a dad's socket set will always be missing the 10-millimeter socket. Dang kids. It's probably in the yard somewhere getting rained on.

30. No matter how organized he is overall, a dad will also have a chaotic junk drawer. Every time he opens it he will complain he can't find anything in this house. But it's all probably in there, somewhere.

· YARD AND MOWING ·

31. A dad raking leaves in his yard will do both of the following:
   a. complain about how many leaves there are this year and how long this will take
   b. make the task much longer for himself by encouraging the kids to jump into the leaf piles before he bags them up. And you know he's gonna jump in them too.

32. A dad will take great pride in his lawn. Even if his family says he is "obsessed," or "weirdly competitive," or that it "literally doesn't matter, it's just grass," he will not be swayed from striving to have the best lawn on the block.

33. A dad will begin mowing his lawn before 7:00 a.m. on a Saturday and not care if the rest of the house (or neighborhood) complains.

34. After the first mow of spring, a dad will stand on his deck with his arms folded admiring the grass. This is peak dad.

35. A dad will view mowing lines in the grass as a thing of beauty and artistry.

36. A dad noticing his grass is a bit too long will comment, "The lawn isn't going to mow itself."

37. A dad watering the lawn or garden will spray the window of the house if a kid is watching from inside to startle them and get a giggle.

DAD AT PLAY

· RELAXATION MODE ·

01. A dad entering relaxation mode will ceremoniously "crack open a cold one."

02. Typical places for a dad to relax include:
  a. a driveway (literally anyone's)
  b. a hammock
  c. the recliner ("his spot" in the living room; see Section XV, Article 1)

· IN THE WATER ·

03. A dad in a swimming pool or other body of water will tell any passersby, "Come on in, the water's fine."

04. A dad who owns a swimming pool will hang a sign that says, "We don't swim in your toilet, so don't pee in our pool." If his spouse objects to the possession or display of the sign, he will simply say this statement out loud whenever guests come to the pool. (Alternate: "Welcome to our OOL. Notice there is no *P* in it. Let's keep it that way.")

05. It's a dad's responsibility to launch kids into the air and/or throw kids around playfully when he is in a pool. He will begin with his own kids, but must also be willing to do

05. this to any random neighborhood kids that start lining up.
(cont.) It is the duty of Fun Pool Dad.

06. A dad swimming in the ocean with his kids will pretend to spot a shark in order to freak them out.

07. A dad who owns a boat will:

    a. name it with a pun (i.e., "Aboat Time," "Pier Pressure," etc.)

    b. bring it up often

    c. treat it like another child

    d. offer to take anyone/everyone out on the boat

    e. take out his aggression on whoever is riding on the tube behind his boat by attempting to bounce them off

    f. call himself "The Captain"

    g. offer everyone a chance to drive the boat (but hover closely)

· HOBBIES ·

08. A dad looks forward to sharing all of his favorite things with his kids and is wildly happy if/when the kids like them too. This includes:

    a. favorite films and books from his childhood

    b. classic video games

    c. specific sports or teams

08.
(cont.)
  d. outdoor activities

  e. favorite bands/music

  f. favorite places (e.g., theme parks, national parks, etc.)

  g. favorite toys (e.g., LEGO, Lincoln Logs, *Star Wars* toys, Hot Wheels, model airplanes, etc.)

09. A dad must never let his child win at Mario Kart, even if the child cries. Mario Kart, like life, won't go easy on you just because you're new here. Oh, you got hit by two red shells on the last lap? My boss hit me with two metaphorical "blue shells" at 5:00 p.m. today at work. Life comes at you fast.

10. A dad will refer to the popular video game Fortnite as "fork knife" to make his teenager cringe. A dad will try playing a new video game just to bond with his kid and may end up really liking it.

11. Even if a dad actually enjoys Fortnite or other games his kid likes too, he'll never turn down an opportunity to tell them how good GoldenEye was on Nintendo 64 and how it paved the way for modern multiplayer video games.

12. A dad will take the Pinewood Derby very seriously and likely care more about winning than the kid does. This same attitude also applies to science fairs because he wants that blue ribbon this year.

13. After doing any amount of activity, a dad will joke that he's done his cardio for the day.

· SPORTS ·

14. Many dads are into sports, but it is not required by Dad Law. If a dad is not a sports dad, he will condescendingly refer to all sports as "sports ball." (A non-sports dad is exempt from the following laws and may skip to the next section.)

15. A dad will show an interest in golf. If not playing it, then watching it. If not watching it, then sleeping on the couch with it on in the background. If none of these things, then at least destroying his family in miniature golf.

16. A dad will have one NFL team he likes and one he hates with an undying passion.

17. A dad will refer to his local sports team as if he's a part of it if they are winning (e.g., "We made the playoffs!"). If they are losing, he will distance himself (e.g., "You believe these guys?").

18. A dad will regularly retell stories from his glory days of playing sports in high school and/or college. He will never tire of telling these stories, even if his family has long since tired of hearing them.

19. A dad playing pool (billiards) is required to attempt the shoot-behind-the-back move. If he pulls it off, he's gonna look so cool.

20. While participating in sports, a dad will say:
     a. after a bad throw on their part: "Ya gotta catch those."
     b. after a mild/moderate success:
         i.   "The old man's still got it."
         ii. "What do you think about your old dad now?"
         iii. "In your face."
         iv. "Put that in your pipe and smoke it."

21. A dad attempting to teach a kid any sport will say, "Keep your eye on the ball." This is the main/only good advice a dad will give, and it will solve any sports-related problem. Probably.

22. A dad will say, "Good arm!" to a kid who throws them something, even if the kid definitely doesn't have a good arm.

23. A dad will shout, "Go long!" before tossing a ball over a fence. You can't be mad at him; he told you to go long.

24. A dad will always remind you it's not whether you win or lose, it's how you play the game.

25. A dad will use talking about fantasy football as a small talk icebreaker with a guy he just met. Who doesn't want to talk about fantasy football? Who doesn't want to hear how early a dad's idiot friend drafted a kicker? (Turns out, a lot of people. But it's worth a shot to make a dad friend.)

26. A dad will tell you they're only good at golf/bowling/pool/darts in the "two-to-four beer range." Might need to get this man another beer.

27. The Super Bowl is to be respected as a dad holiday.

    a. A dad will treat a Super Bowl party like a second Thanksgiving, but instead of turkey, he overeats nachos and wings. He will never skimp on Super Bowl snacks. This is no time for moderation.

    b. The dad who brings the best snack to the Super Bowl party will be acknowledged "the man."

    c. A veggie tray will be served along with the good snacks but will remain largely untouched. The important thing is that it's there.

    d. A dad will complain about the halftime show.

    e. A dad will have strong opinions about the commercials.

28. A dad will run a Super Bowl squares operation and give squares to their kids for free when not enough people sign up.

29. A dad will talk about their March Madness bracket strategy to whoever will listen. Nearly every year at least one twelve seed upsets a five seed. Isn't that amazing? (Just nod.)

DAD ENTERTAINMENT

· SEATING ·

01. A dad will have a spot in the living room (preferably a chair of a reclining nature) that is designated as "his spot."

    a. If a kid is found to be in his spot, Dad Law states that the kid must relinquish the spot to the dad. Move it or lose it, pal.

02. A dad moving from a standing position to a sitting position (or vice versa) will make a series of grunts. These grunts are vital to the process of sitting down/getting up.

03. If a dad is comfortably sitting down but needs a drink, he will wait for someone to walk by and ask them to bring him a drink. He will preface this request with, "Since you're up."

    a. In the event that no one is already up, a dad may manufacture an excuse to make someone get up (e.g., "Go let the dog out, son."). He will then take this opportunity to use the "Since you're up" procedure. It's foolproof.

04. If a dad isn't lying on the couch or sitting in his spot, he's often found watching TV standing up with his arms folded. This commonly occurs during tense moments in televised sporting events. The standing position improves his vantage point and gives him better opportunity to pace and shout, "Ya gotta catch those!"

05. If a child is standing in front of the TV and blocking a dad's view, he will state one of the following:

    a. "You make a better door than a window."

    b. "Your father was not a glassmaker."

    c. "You may be a pane but you're not a window."

· MOVIES ·

06. A dad will hold a special place in his heart for sports movies, and he will not be shamed or mocked when he inevitably cries at the end of *Rudy*. (See Section IX, Article 62 on crying.)

07. A dad climbing a large staircase will hum the *Rocky* theme song. Failure to do so would be a blatant violation of Dad Law and an utter waste of a staircase.

08. A dad will refer to a movie as a "flick" (e.g., "Oh, *Caddyshack*. I love this flick.").

09. A dad will quote the same line from his favorite movie/TV show for way longer than it is relevant or funny. He can't help himself; it's a part of his brain now.

    a. If the line is from a show or movie that came out before a kid was born, a dad will explain the entirety of the movie plot to the kid any time he uses the line.

09. **b.** The line will most likely be from one of the following:
(cont.)
    i. *SNL* sketches from thirty years ago

    ii. Monty Python

    iii. *The Simpsons*

    iv. *Borat*

    v. any film with Bill Murray, Steve Martin, Adam Sandler, or Jim Carrey

10. A dad will always have a very firm opinion on which is better: *Star Wars* or *Star Trek*. There is a right answer, but he must find it within himself.

11. A dad who enjoys *Star Wars* will take any chance to discuss it, including one or more of the following:

a. how much he hates the prequel films, especially Jar Jar Binks

b. a ranking of the films according to his opinion of their quality

c. saying, "I am your father" in a Darth Vader voice with optional use of his mask sounds

d. saying, "Do or do not. There is no try," or attempting to make up his own phrases in Yoda-speak

e. the virtues of Baby Yoda

f. obscure planet details and character backstories

12. A dad will complain about how many movie remakes there are these days. He will wonder why they don't have any original ideas in Hollywood anymore. However, he's not about to pass up a Spider-Man or James Bond flick.

13. A dad at a movie theater will (loudly) complain that the snacks are absurdly overpriced. It's practically criminal. (See Section IV, Article 18 on highway robbery.)

14. A dad will buy a large popcorn with butter at the movies despite it being so offensively expensive because, "What's a movie without popcorn?"

15. The classic dad movies to show to their kids way before the kids are even close to mature enough to view them include:
  a. *The Godfather*
  b. *Die Hard*
  c. *Caddyshack*
  d. *Braveheart*
  e. *The Blues Brothers*
  f. *Rambo: First Blood*
  g. *Predator*
  h. *Airplane!*
  i. *The Terminator*
  j. *Planes, Trains and Automobiles*

16. A dad will watch any/all movies featuring Tom Hanks in any capacity. Tom Hanks is the unofficial movie mascot of the dads.

17. A dad will take any opportunity to say, "I'll be bahk," in an Arnold Schwarzenegger voice.

18. If a dad hears anyone say, "Surely you can't be serious," he will automatically state, "I am serious, and don't call me Shirley."

19. A dad cannot resist a good war documentary or film, including all wars but especially World War II. He will also recount any family stories of veterans whenever possible.

· MUSIC ·

20. A dad listening to any new music he doesn't care for will call it "noise" or "racket." He may try to give it a chance, for his kids' sake, but it takes Herculean strength to not complain about it.

21. A dad listening to classic rock will say, "Now *this* is music."

XV · DAD ENTERTAINMENT

22. A dad watching the Grammy Awards or listening to anything on the radio will complain that he doesn't recognize any of the artists anymore. He will assure his kids that even though he's lame now, he was cool, once.

23. A dad will deliberately (and sometimes accidentally) get the names of modern bands incorrect (e.g., "Is this Blink 195?"). This is done to elicit a laugh or groan from the kids, and to communicate that he knows he's out of the loop but doesn't care. Dads will also apply the same technique to song lyrics.

24. A dad is required to do an air drum solo when listening to that one part of Phil Collins's "In the Air Tonight." If he's driving when it comes on, that steering wheel's gonna get it.

25. A dad will have one goofy trademark dance move that he's ready to pull out at any time. After doing it, he will always declare he's "still got it" and look around to see whether anyone is impressed.

26. A dad will say that music was better "back in the day." Exactly what "day" that was depends on the age of the dad but is definitely a time way before his kids were born.

27.   A dad will have one favorite album that he listens to on at least a weekly basis for his entire adult life. His kids may complain about having to hear it all the time, but one day they will feel great nostalgia tied to that particular album because it reminds them of their dad.

28.   *A dad is permitted to purchase one or more expensive instruments (preferably a guitar) to display in his home. Whether or not he intends to ever actually play the thing is irrelevant.*

29.   A dad hearing a familiar song will inform everyone around him if he used to know how to play this song on the guitar. Common songs for a dad to know how to play on the guitar include but are not limited to:

    a.   Green Day, "Good Riddance (Time of Your Life)"

29.
(cont.)

    b. Tom Petty, "Free Fallin'"

    c. Led Zeppelin, "Stairway to Heaven"

    d. the intros to several old Metallica songs

30. If a dad is really feeling a song, he will play air guitar or drum on the steering wheel at stoplights.

31. A happy dad will dance, sing, and enjoy his music however he wants, without caring whether it embarrasses his kids. A dancing dad is nature's most majestic creature.

DAD AT WORK

· AT-HOME DADS ·

01. All dads are "working dads." Stay-at-home dads may be the hardest working of all.

· COWORKER INTERACTIONS ·

02. When a dad sees a coworker he must always ask, "Workin' hard, or hardly workin'?" It is on record as being funny every single time.

03. A dad who encounters a coworker out in the wild (not at work) will say one of the following:
  a. "You broke free, huh?"
  b. "Hey, get back to work!"
  c. "Playing hooky?"

04. A dad will call chatting with coworkers "shooting the breeze." He loves shooting the breeze on company time.

05. If someone is eating lunch in a common area, it is illegal for a dad to not comment on this. He will enthusiastically state one of the following:
  a. "That smells good."
  b. "Bring enough for all of us?"
  c. "Looks better than what I'm havin'."

06. When someone is eating at work, a dad must announce the name of the food to the entire office. For example, he may state, "Eating some yogurt, huh?" or, "What's that? A turkey sandwich? Mustard, interesting."

07. In the rare event of a perfect work joke setup, when someone asks, "How many people work here?" a dad must maintain his composure before sticking the landing on the punch line: "About half."

08. If a dad encounters a coworker leaving work as he's going in to work, no matter what time it is, he's required to say one of the following:

    a. "You're goin' the wrong way."
    b. "Banking hours?"
    c. "Thanks for coming in."

· WORK HABITS ·

09. Dads under the age of thirty-five who work in an office must maintain a collection of quirky dress socks, all of which are unique. Dads over the age of thirty-five must wear the same type of dress sock every day, because they buy it in bulk. (See Section VIII, Article 4 on sock buying.)

10. A dad giving work advice will always suggest one or more of the following generic work phrases he got off an inspirational poster hanging in his office:
    a. "Always give 110 percent."
    b. "Go above and beyond."
    c. "Go the extra mile."
    d. "Be the first one there and the last to leave."
    e. "Be a team player."
    f. "Play hardball."
    g. "Swing for the fences."

11. If a dad is asked how he's doing on a Monday, he will respond, "Not bad for a Monday." Mondays are, on average, 60 percent worse than every other day.

12. A dad introducing a lot of people must joke that there will be a quiz later.

13. A dad will say, "Having fun yet?" to a group of people who are clearly not having fun.

14. If a dad observes that two of his coworkers are wearing the same color shirt, he will comment, "Guess I didn't get the memo!" (Depending on the age of the dad, this may be meant as an actual joke or used ironically.)

15. If a coworker asks a dad how his weekend was, he is required to respond, "Not long enough." It was never long enough, Ted. Stop asking.

16. A dad will ask his coworkers whether they caught the big game. Letting a big game pass without discussing it at work is a violation of Dad Law.

· BUZZWORDS AND OFFICE LINGO ·

17. A dad will describe anything he deems too flashy but lacking in substance as "a dog and pony show." Frankly, a dog and pony show sounds awesome, but a dad means it in a negative way.

18. A dad may describe his work environment as "cutthroat" on hard days. On good days, however, he may refer to his coworkers as his second family. (You can tell it's his second family because he's started telling them not to touch the thermostat. See Section I, Article 1.)

19. A dad in possession of a #1 Dad mug will use it at work. In the event that a dad does not have one, he should first reflect internally on why this may be: *Get it together, man.* Then, he may use a mug with a pun or other humorous statement (e.g., "Don't talk to me before I've had my coffee," or a *Far Side* comic).

20. A dad going back to work after a break of any duration will say he's going "back to the salt mines." It's always a salt mine, which is widely accepted as the worst of the mines.

21. A dad will describe a coworker as being "in the trenches" with him. A dad is forever loyal to someone who has been in the trenches with him.

22. A dad may describe higher-ups in his company as "the suits." He both resents and respects the suits, depending on the day. One day he may become one of the suits, in which case he will retire the term.

23. A dad will refer to his boss (behind the boss's back) as either "boss man/boss lady" or by an unaffectionate nickname, not suitable to be printed here.

24. A dad working late will say he's:
    a. "burning the midnight oil"
    b. "burning the candle at both ends"
    c. "in crunch time"
    d. "working my fingers to the bone"

25. A dad will refer to future ventures as being:
    a. in the pipeline
    b. on the horizon
    c. in the planning stage

26. A dad will refer to working as "bringing home the bacon." Bacon is one of the most important things a dad could ever bring home, after all.

27. A dad ready to work will announce one of the following:
  a. "Let's roll up our sleeves."
  b. "Let's get down to brass tacks."
  c. "Let's get down to the nitty-gritty."
  d. "Let's get the ball rolling."
  e. "Let's get our hands dirty."

28. A dad will take every opportunity to remind his family, "A little hard work never killed anyone." He may also need to remind himself of this, on exhausting days.

29. A dad with an idea that was proven unsuccessful will say one of the following:
  a. "Looks like it's back to the drawing board."
  b. "Looks like we're back at square one."
  c. "You gotta kiss a few frogs before you find a prince."
  d. "Nothing ventured, nothing gained."
  e. "Rome wasn't built in a day."

30. A dad at work will refer to the period of time between any two things as "the interim." He will repeat this word in the interim between the start of the interim and the completion of the interim.

31. If a coworker says, "See you later," a dad will respond with, "Thanks for the warning."

32. A dad will say, "I'm not as dumb as I look," after saying something that's not very dumb.

33. A dad will say, "I see what you did there," if he sees what you did there.

34. A dad at work will complain daily about one or more of the following:
    a. all the red tape
    b. all the hoops he has to jump through
    c. the rat race
    d. all the meetings that could have been an email

35. A dad will refer to someone who has been fired as:
    a. sacked
    b. shown the door
    c. given the old heave-ho
    d. adiosed
    e. given the pink slip

36. A dad will keep a photo of his family in his workspace as a reminder of why he does all this work in the first place.

DAD ON VACATION

· PREPARATIONS ·

01. A dad packing for vacation will:
   a. complain about how much luggage the family has
   b. say that trying to fit it all in the back of the car is like Tetris, which luckily he is an expert at
   c. ask the owner of a heavy bag, "What you got in here? Rocks?"
   d. worry about the baggage weight limit when flying, repeatedly lifting the bag and squinting in an attempt to weigh it with his brain

02. A dad will start loading up the car many hours before leaving on a trip, and it will always take longer than he expects.

· ROAD TRIPS ·

03. Before leaving town on a road trip, a dad will top off his gas tank so he can go as long as possible without stopping once they hit the road.

04. A dad on a road trip will buy snacks consisting entirely of junk food as if he's a kid again. There are no nutritional rules or guidelines on road trips. It's total snack anarchy for the duration of the drive.

05. In the event that a kid has to pee on a road trip but the dad doesn't want to stop, he will ask them to "hold it until the next state."

06. If a dad needs to pee on a road trip, he cannot tell anyone. This would show weakness in the man who said, "We're not stopping until Kansas!" Instead, he must wait until someone else needs to go, and then complain about having to stop as if it is an inconvenience to him.

· AIR TRAVEL ·

07. A dad will print his boarding pass days in advance. He will double-check that he has his printed copy before walking out the door, then triple-check, then check a few more times just to be safe. You can't trust mobile apps.

08. A dad will get to the airport at least four hours early because you never know.

09. A dad on a flight will become best friends with the person sitting next to him before the flight is over. He may also get an invitation to visit the guy's cabin out in Tahoe sometime.

· BEACH VACATIONS ·

10. A dad at the beach will assist his kids with building a sandcastle, often with accompanying moat. He will also allow the children to bury him in sand up to his head if they ask.

11. A dad at the beach will help his kids find shells or sea creatures.

12. A dad leaving the beach will complain that there's sand everywhere. He will moan that they'll be finding it for weeks. Aaaand now it's all over the back seat of the car.

· ZOOS ·

13. A dad at the zoo will say one or more of the following:
    a. "Whoa, it's a zoo in here!" upon entering
    b. "This place is for the birds" when entering the bird sanctuary. He's been saving this one in his back pocket all day.
    c. "Don't fall in!" at every animal enclosure
    d. "Look, it's you!" (pointing at any goofy-looking animal)

13.   **e.** "You forget how big they are." (When viewing any
(cont.)   large animal. Of course, he knew giraffes were big,
            but he forgot how big. Really tall. Look at that neck.)

         f. "This guy's got the right idea!" (upon seeing an animal
            eating or napping, which is what he wishes he were
            doing right now)

· MUSEUMS ·

14.   A dad on vacation will insist upon visiting at least one
historical or educational site per trip, even if/when the
kids groan.

15.   A dad at a museum will show appropriate interest by
reading plaques aloud to his children. He may even add,
"Well, isn't that interesting!" His interest in each exhibit is
inversely proportional to the amount of time they've been
at the museum. By the end of the visit he'll be speeding
through entire rooms, but at the beginning he's sure into
appreciating each individual artifact at length.

· PHOTOGRAPHY ·

16.   If a dad is asked to take a photo for someone, he will do
one or all of the following:

16.
(cont.)

   a. struggle with figuring out the camera on the phone. He may unintentionally take a selfie while trying to take the real photo. (Advanced dads will purposefully take a selfie to leave on the other person's camera roll for them to find.)

   b. ask them to say anything but "cheese" (e.g., "Saaaay 'family time!'")

   c. say, "That's a keeper."

   d. say, "That's a framer."

17. After someone takes his photo, a dad will ask, "Did you get my good side?" This is a trick question, as all sides of a dad are very good.

· VACATION EXPENSES ·

18. A dad who wanted and planned a vacation will still complain about the cost of said vacation.

19. A dad will resist any member of the family spending money in overpriced gift shops while on vacation.

20. A dad visiting an amusement park will complain about the price of admission but become like a kid again on the rides. He may have a crusty adult exterior but he's young at heart.

21.   A dad at Disneyland/Disney World will express how outrageous the prices are at least once per hour. He will likely make a sarcastic comment about "the happiest place on earth." After buying food, he will increase his complaint frequency to once per minute for the subsequent hour.

22.   A dad in a nice place or on a nice vacation will say, "I could get used to this." He really could.

DAD ON HOLIDAYS

· GIFTS ·

01. Any celebration that includes the giving or receiving of gifts requires a dad to:

    a. be standing at the ready with a garbage bag. He must immediately collect the discarded wrapping paper the moment it hits the ground, even if it disrupts the alleged "fun."

    b. collect and save any boxes deemed to be "really good boxes." Don't just throw those away; you can reuse them.

02. A dad will give his spouse a present on all holidays and occasions, even (and especially) if the spouse has stated no presents need be exchanged this time. A smart dad knows that's a trap.

03. After giving a gift, a dad will proudly inform the recipient of the number of stars the item has on its Amazon rating. He wouldn't buy you any old 3.5-star-rated gift, no sir.

04. A dad will give a random (often unnecessary) tool as a gift and then regularly ask the person whether they are using it for years to come. He'll be checking up on it. If you aren't using it, he will tell you that you should. If you are using it, he will brag that he told you you'd use it.

05.   A dad is responsible for assembling any/all large gifts (including, but not limited to, bikes, dollhouses, and play kitchens).

06.   A dad assembling a large toy or piece of furniture is not required to read the instructions first. The text stating "Please read all instructions before assembling" is intended for amateurs, not dads.

07.   In any gift giving/receiving situation, a dad may be called upon as an IT consultant to set up all electronics.

· BIRTHDAYS ·

08.   When his birthday is approaching, a dad will inform his family:
   a.   not to spend money on him
   b.   that he doesn't need anything
   c.   about the expensive tech thing he really needs

09.   If there's a perfect gift for a dad's birthday that the family is secretly planning to buy for him, he will go ahead and buy it for himself, a week before his birthday. Happens every time.

10.   A dad will tell people, "You're that young? I've got T-shirts older than you!" on their birthday.

11.   On a child's birthday, a dad will ask him or her, "Feel any different?"

· PARTIES ·

12.   A dad at a child's birthday party is required to do one or more of the following:
- **a.** go into the bouncy castle with the kids. The sign saying "No Adults Allowed" does not apply to dads.
- **b.** watch the kids running around and remark to the nearest adult, "I wish I had their energy."
- **c.** joke about the sugar crash the kids will have soon
- **d.** make friends with any nearby dads by asking, "You belong to one of these kids?"
- **e.** congratulate the birthday boy or girl on reaching "The Big (insert child's age)" (e.g., "There he is, the birthday boy. How does it feel to be the big one-oh!?")
- **f.** make the hilarious remark that it seems like just a year ago we were celebrating the last birthday

13.   On his spouse's birthday, a dad will do one or more of the following:
- **a.** insist the spouse "keeps getting younger"
- **b.** say he doesn't know how she puts up with him
- **c.** proudly respond, "That's why I married her," when someone says something nice about her

14. On his own birthday, a dad will tell everyone he's turning twenty-nine again. It will be less funny every year.

· HALLOWEEN ·

15. A dad is responsible for overseeing the carving of pumpkins, whether he wants to or not. He will help with removal of all pumpkin guts and finishing the jack-o'-lanterns after the kids get tired of it. This applies even if he originally said he didn't want to carve pumpkins this year because he always ends up doing all the work. Too bad, it's festive.

16. After trick-or-treating on Halloween, a dad is entitled to enforce a "dad tax" of:
    a. several fun-size candy bars of his favorite type
    b. one full-size candy bar of his favorite type
    Once the child has left the candy unattended for more than two minutes, a dad may sneak even more candy for himself as long as the amount is not noticed by the child.

17. A dad will guess a kid's Halloween costume wrong on purpose to make the kid laugh. He may also tease, "That's a scary mask," to a kid who is not wearing a mask at all.

· THANKSGIVING ·

18. A dad on Thanksgiving will bathe in the glory of being the one to carve the turkey. It is a treasured dad moment.

19. A dad on Thanksgiving will say he "knows how the turkey feels" when he's "stuffed" after dinner.

20. A dad will often proclaim that he "can't quit cold turkey" while eating Thanksgiving leftovers.

21. A dad who dislikes shopping on any other day will get really into Black Friday deals (especially on electronics). You'd be crazy to pass on this kind of deal.

· CHRISTMAS ·

22. A dad is responsible for the hanging of holiday lights on the tree and exterior of the home. He is also required to fix or untangle all strands of lights. He is rewarded with the glory of being the one to turn on the lights for the first time. He is paid only in impressed oohs and ahhs from his family. Worth it.

23. A dad's favorite Christmas film will be either:
   a. *National Lampoon's Christmas Vacation*
   b. *Die Hard*

24. If a dad says he's going to play "Christmas music," the first song he plays must be one of the following:

    a. "Grandma Got Run Over by a Reindeer"

    b. "The Chanukah Song" by Adam Sandler

    c. a metal Christmas song by Trans-Siberian Orchestra

25. A dad will use the threat "Santa is watching!" as a replacement for parenting during the months leading up to Christmas. He may even threaten to call Santa and tell him about a particular situation if the kid is misbehaving. The Elf on the Shelf may be called in for reinforcements.

26. A dad will track Santa's location via the NORAD tracker on Christmas Eve.

27. Christmas Eve is the one day a year that a dad will wear matching pajamas with his family without complaining.

· NEW YEAR'S EVE/DAY ·

28. At the beginning of each calendar year, a dad will make a minimum of five "I haven't seen you since last year" jokes per day.

29. When asked about New Year's resolutions, a dad will state that his resolution is not to make any resolutions. He may also add a clarifying clause about not messing with perfection.

30. A dad on New Year's Eve is permitted to play the prerecorded ball drop from last year if it means getting the kids to go to bed earlier. Staying up until midnight is a young man's game.

· FOURTH OF JULY ·

31. A dad will coordinate a big cookout for the Fourth of July and individually ask each guest whether they want a burger or a hot dog.

32. A dad becomes like a reckless, giddy teenager when it comes to buying and setting off fireworks on the Fourth of July.

· MISCELLANEOUS HOLIDAYS ·

33. A dad will always complain that the stores put out holiday decorations too early and it seems to get earlier every year.

34. A dad on Saint Patrick's Day will attempt an Irish accent that ends up sounding exactly like the Lucky Charms leprechaun.

35. A dad on Easter will hide eggs in impossible-to-find places and then forget about them until they are discovered months later.

36. A dad on Father's Day will love every gift he receives, even if he already has enough ties.

DAD AT REST

· FALLING ASLEEP ·

01. A dad who sits down on the couch for any amount of time will fall asleep, snore loudly, and then claim, "I was just resting my eyes."

02. A dad who is asleep on the couch in front of the TV will suddenly wake up if you change the channel and claim, "I was watching that."

03. A dad at rest shall remain at rest until acted upon by outside forces. These forces may be a child jumping on him and kneeing him in the nuts, a baby crying, a child shouting for a snack, or any other arbitrary domestic want, need, desire, or whim that comes up at any given time. In other words, a dad at rest shall not remain at rest for long.

04. A dad who is going to bed will say he's:
   a. "hitting the sack"
   b. "calling it a day"
   c. "turning in"

05. A dad deciding to go to bed will announce to his family that he needs to turn in because he has work in the morning. Everyone already knows he has work in the morning. It doesn't need to be said, but he will say it anyway.

06. A dad will respect naptime as a sacred time. (Naptime for the kids, and for himself. Nothing gets between a dad and his nap.)

07. A dad of young children will stay up late after his kids are in bed, no matter how tired he may be, because it's the only time he gets to himself to watch TV, play video games, or do nothing but exist as he is, not just as someone's parent.

08. An exhausted dad will keep on trucking, stating simply, "I'll sleep when I'm dead." That may not be too far off actually. At least when it comes to sleeping in greater than eight-hour increments.

· GETTING UP ·

09. A dad will brag about how early he got up this morning. The earlier a dad gets up, the more he will brag.

10. A dad on vacation will still wake up early, even though he doesn't have to. It's a point of pride, and his body has completely forgotten how to sleep in anyway.

11. A dad who has had a particularly productive morning will tell everyone that he gets more done before 9:00 a.m. than most people do all day.

12. A dad waking a child for the day will use one or more of the following phrases:
    a. "Rise and shine."
    b. "Up and at 'em."
    c. "Good morning, sunshine."
    d. "Good morning, sleeping beauty."
    e. "Wakey, wakey, eggs and bakey."
    f. "C'mon, we're burnin' daylight."

13. If a kid sleeps past 8:00 a.m., even if it's not the dad's own kid, a dad must respond with one of the following:
    a. "Good afternoon."
    b. "Nice of you to join us."
    c. "Well, look who's back from the dead."

14. A dad will tell early risers, "The early bird gets the worm."

15. On the other hand, a dad will tell late risers, "The last mouse gets the cheese."

16. If his kids are being too loud in the morning, a dad will tell them they are "waking the whole neighborhood," which is apparently a great offense. However, this same principle inexplicably does not apply to a dad when he decides to mow his lawn at 7:00 a.m. (See Section XIII, Article 33 on early morning mowing.)

· AFTERWORD ·

Dad Law is comprehensive and unchanging. While all that is contained within this volume may seem overwhelming to a new dad, he will soon find that many, if not all, dad laws come naturally to him.

The moment he laced up his white sneakers and struggled to install the car seat for the first time, he joined a worldwide community of dads doing their best for their families and making jokes while doing it. He must learn to follow the dad compass inside himself.

Most importantly, he will come to understand that the spirit of Dad Law is simple. Every law boils down to a few innate governing principles.

The core of Dad Law is that a dad will show love for his family by:

    a. trying to make them laugh (even if it comes with some eye rolls)

    b. imparting life lessons (even if the audience is less than enthusiastic at the time)

    c. taking care of practical matters (even if everyone is tired of being asked about the oil in their car)

    d. creating happy memories with his spouse and kids

    e. being present physically, mentally, and emotionally for the family that means everything to him

· ACKNOWLEDGMENTS ·

Compiling a comprehensive collection of Dad Law was an ambitious and probably crazy undertaking. It couldn't have happened without a heroic team effort and a lot of in-depth consultations with dad behavior experts (a term we just made up for people who like dad jokes).

Special thanks to *The Dad* team of hilarious contributing writers, especially Jimmy Applegath, Marion Boyd, Morgan Music, and Jordan Stratton, who helped us transcribe the sacred laws upon these pages.

Thank you to the Some Spider team, especially Adam Hawkin, Phuong Ireland, Lindsey Martin, Merin Pasternak, and Julie Steinhagen, and everyone who helped make this important legal volume a reality.

The world thanks you.